BEGINNER'S GUIDE TO
GETTING PUBLISHED

COMPLETELY REVISED AND UPDATED

FROM THE EDITORS OF WRITER'S DIGEST BOOKS

WRITER'S DIGEST BOOKS
CINCINNATI, OHIO

Beginners Guide to Getting Published. Copyright © 1994 by Writer's Digest
Books. Printed and bound in the United States of America. All rights reserved. No
part of this book may be reproduced in any form or by any electronic or mechanical
means including information storage and retrieval systems without permission in
writing from the publisher, except by a reviewer, who may quote brief passages in a
review. Published by Writer's Digest Books, an imprint of F&W Publications, Inc.,
1507 Dana Avenue, Cincinnati, Ohio, 45207. 1-800-289-0963. Second edition.

98 97 96 95 94   5 4 3 2 1

Library of Congress Cataloging in Publication Data

Beginners guide to getting published.
       p.   cm.
    Includes index.
    ISBN 0-89879-672-5
    1. Authorship—Marketing. 2. Publishers and publishing—United States.
    I. Writer's Digest Books (Firm)
PN161.B444   1994
808'.02—dc20   94-11186
                                                                                CIP

Project Coordinator: David Tompkins
Interior Design: Angela Lennert
Cover Design: Ben Ross

The permissions on the next page constitute an extension of this copyright page.

PERMISSIONS

PREFACE

We last published this invaluable guide for the beginning writer in 1987. The revised version now in your hands updates the core articles of its successful predecessor and replaces other pieces with advice-filled articles published in *Writer's Digest* in the years since *Beginner's Guide to Getting Published* last appeared. This expanded edition provides concrete and immediately useful tips to help you get published.

The first part of this guide inspires you to get moving on your writing projects. Experienced authors relate their experiences as neophytes and share what motivated them. You'll see that age is no hindrance to those who want to write.

The second section offers practical advice on getting published. You'll learn how to prepare the manuscripts you'll soon be sending out and how to compose the all-important query letter. Two widely published authors will then give you step-by-step plans to make your dream of seeing your words in print come true.

The third and largest section details the different markets open to the aspiring writer. The section starts with smaller opportunities, such as fillers or newspaper columns, to help you build your clip file and gain experience. Other markets, such as greeting cards, poetry and book reviews, are also explored. You'll also find advice from established experts in the areas of travel, hobby and business writing. Finally, you will get advice on the ever more feasible option of self-publishing.

The fourth section shows you how to make the leap into the Big Time. You'll learn how to establish the important rapport with editors. Other articles show you how to widen your scope from local to national to international. You'll learn to plumb your expanding files for resale possibilities even as you aim for the bestseller list. Then, you'll get advice on when to make the important decision to become a full-time writer.

And, finally, you'll get to hear how one writer derives satisfaction outside the realm of sales.

This book provides a necessary framework to get you started on your career as a writer. To keep abreast of other opportunities and for more advice, consult *Writer's Digest* magazine. And to stay informed of the ever-changing markets, refer to *Writer's Market*.

We look forward to seeing your name in print!

The editors of Writer's Digest Books

I.

General Inspiration

We Were All Beginners Once

Lawrence Block

One of the first things a writer is asked by a new acquaintance is if he has ever had anything published. There was a time when this irked me, until I saw it as a natural enough way of establishing one's professional status, or lack thereof. One may be a painter without being hung or a traitor without being hanged; similarly, one may be a writer without being published, but one cannot be a *real* writer, so, er, ahem, *have* you had anything published, Mr. Block?

Indeed I have, I'll assure my new friend. I've been supporting myself with my typewriter ever since college. I've made, certainly, a better living in some years than in others, but I've always scraped by. And as for being published, I was still in college when my first books and stories saw print.

My conversational partner will nod at this, grateful to know he or she is not in the presence of an imposter, a writer *manqué*. Then a sullen glaze will come into his or her eyes.

"You read about the struggle writers have to get published. The years of heartbreak. The endless rounds of rejection slips. The poverty, the menial jobs. But you, you never had any of that, did you?"

Didn't I? "Oh, it was all ages ago," I'll say, "back around the time of Columbus's second voyage. So it's really pretty hard to remember."

Hard to remember? It might have been yesterday.

All I wanted during my first year at college was to be published. I'd decided a couple of years earlier that I intended to become a writer. How was one to manage that? By majoring in English, I supposed, and by reading everything I could lay my eyes on, and, finally, by sitting down at the typewriter and actually writing something.

And then submitting it, whatever it might be. Poems, sketches, three- and four-page short stories. I'd blush to recall the adolescent tripe I had the gall to submit for publication, but for the arrogance implicit in such a blush. Publishers, I now know, are forever inundated with unsuitable, amateurish submissions. My efforts were not even outstanding in their unsuitability, in their amateurishness. I'm sure they were examined and rejected and returned in short order, leaving no impression on the poor slush reader's mind once they'd left his hands.

I remember one of those stories. It was about two feral children in a scientific experiment. There's a global war or some comparable calamity and only those two infants survive. So they grow up and mate and have two children, and they call one Cain and the other Abel.

Oh, dear. I was to learn that every magazine gets that story two or three times a week. And even if that wasn't the case, what I'd written wasn't a story. It was just a gimmick afloat on a thousand-word ocean.

And where did I send it? *Harper's Magazine*, *The Atlantic Monthly*, *The New Yorker*. Places like that.

Well, what do you want? I was a beginner. I didn't know any better.

In an autobiography, *Call It Experience*, Erskine Caldwell tells of his first sale. The future author of *God's Little Acre* and *Tobacco Road* had written some earthy stories about poor folks in red-dirt Georgia. He sent them around and got a letter from Maxwell Perkins at *Scribner's Magazine*. Could Caldwell come to New York to discuss two of his stories?

Caldwell rode up on a bus and Perkins took him to lunch, where they talked about everything but the two stories the young Georgian had sent in. Over coffee, the editor said: "About those two stories, I'd like to publish them. I thought we might pay you two-fifty for the short one and three-fifty for the longer one."

Caldwell looked unhappy. Perkins asked if something was wrong.

"Well, I suppose it's all right," Caldwell allowed, "but I thought I'd be getting more than six dollars for two stories."

The first money I ever got from a publisher was two dollars from a magazine called *Ranch Romances*. Pines Publications issued *Ranch Romances*, and at the time it was the last survivor of a whole string of western pulps. It was, editorially speaking, a bizarre hybrid, featuring love stories on horseback, as it were.

In the summer of 1956, I spent three months working as a mail boy at Pines Publications. When I got back to college, I clipped some newspaper item and sent it to Helen Tono, who was editing *Ranch Romances*. She bought it as a filler and sent me a check for two bucks, along with a note of encouragement. I don't know if she'd have bought it if she hadn't remembered me. Oh, well. It's not what you know, it's who you know. Right?

It was money from a publisher, and that was something. But it wasn't for anything I'd written.

There was something almost schizoid in my attitude, it seems to me. On the one hand, I believed (or thought I believed) that one ought to be prepared to starve for one's art, that a writer's artistic integrity was his most precious possession.

On the other hand, I would have done anything to get published. *Anything.*

It's hard to remember the urgency of my need to see my words in print. I can see now that what a beginner really needs is not to be published but to grow as a writer. The writing I did was valuable to me, but why did I have to send off all my poems and stories?

I suppose the whole process helped me to take myself and my ambitions seriously. Even the rejection slips, tacked neatly to my dorm room wall, seemed to validate what I was doing. They were visible proof that I was engaged in a process aimed at eventual publication.

If I hadn't been submitting things, if I hadn't been trying to get into print, I'm not sure I'd have kept writing.

The first money I received for my own writing was seven dollars from a religious magazine. A friend and I wandered into a Bowery mission one night and watched the down-and-outers endure the service so they could get the meal that followed it. I went home and turned the experience into a 700-word article. "We Found God on the Bowery," I called it, and I told how what began as a lark ended in a conversion experience. "We came to scoff," I wrote, "but we stayed to pray."

That wasn't what happened. Cynical sophomoric wretches we were, we came to scoff and scoffed our way home. But, as I told you, I would have done anything to get published. I submitted my story to a magazine published by the denomination that sponsored the mission. They bought it, printed it and paid for it.

They even used my title.

While I was working as a mail clerk at Pines Publications, I wrote a story about a wise-guy crook who works at a drugstore and steals from his boss, then moves on to mail fraud. The mood was pretty good, but it didn't really make a story. Back at school, I polished the story and sent it to *Manhunt*.

It came back with a note from the editor. He liked it, but it needed a snapper for an ending. If I could think of something, he'd like to look at it again.

I couldn't believe it. I ran out, bought a copy of *Manhunt*, read every story in it, then rewrote mine with a new ending in which the narrator is hoist with his own petard, investing his ill-gotten gains in what the reader can tell is phony uranium stock. It was a hokey notion, and the story came back with another nice note, saying it didn't really work and better luck next time. I wasn't surprised. I hadn't really expected to sell it.

Meanwhile, I had a couple of poems accepted here and there. And I was producing stories regularly for a fiction workshop. And one day I thought of a way to redo my *Manhunt* story. I had the narrator move up another rung and become a contract killer. I was pretty sure it worked this time, and I sent it off, and the editor bought it.

A hundred bucks. It was months before I got the money, more months before the magazine was on the stands. I couldn't wait; I wanted the magazine to be on sale the day after I got the letter of acceptance.

I'm still like that. I want to type THE END, take the last page out of the typewriter, then walk around the corner and see the book on sale in the stores. Don Fine, my publisher at Arbor House, seems to be similarly inclined. He has listed books of mine in his catalog before I've gotten any further than the title, has had covers printed before I've finished the manuscript, and gets the book on the shelves in a fraction of the time most publishers take.

A man after my own heart.

You know what? I'm still a beginner. I've written more books than anyone should have to read, yet every time I hold a new book in my hand I get a thrill not unlike the one I received when I picked up that copy of *Manhunt*. I still try new things, and sometimes they're as ill-advised as my Adam-and-Eve story. I still take chances, and sometimes they work and sometimes they don't. On some level, I still look to publication as a form of validation of who I am and what I do.

In *Cup of Gold*, John Steinbeck's first novel, an old sage said something along these lines to the earnest young hero:

You are young, and want the moon to drink from as a cup of gold. Reaching and straining to catch the moon, you may catch a firefly. But if you grow up you will realize that you cannot have the moon, and would not want it if you could. And you will catch no fireflies.

That's paraphrase; I don't have the book at hand, and it was twenty-five years ago that I read it. There's been a lot of water under the bridge since then, or over the dam, or wherever it goes.

A lot of fireflies, too. Aren't they pretty? And don't they cast a lovely light?

Writing for the Pure Joy of It!

Leonard L. Knott

Dorothy is an old friend of mine who skis, skates, hikes in all kinds of weather and climbs mountains. She also writes poetry. Dorothy doesn't make any money out of any of these activities; she's an all-around amateur — and proud of it.

One night, she came to our house for dinner. I asked what she had been doing all day. "I was up at five this morning, as usual. Did my yoga exercises, went for a two-mile walk, raked the leaves, had my lunch, and sat down and wrote a poem."

The poem was about an early morning on the lakeshore. Sunrises, water ripples, white sand and reflections of trees and clouds are what her poems are all about.

Dorothy has been writing poetry for fifty years or more. One of her poems was published years ago in a poetry magazine; she didn't get paid for it but received some complimentary copies of the magazine.

She has a bit of a reputation as the poet laureate of the suburb where she lives. Should a couple be celebrating a golden wedding anniversary, she's on hand with a sonnet or an ode or just a bit of doggerel commemorating their courtship and their happiness. (I have one framed on my library wall, reminding me that I have enjoyed more than fifty years of wedded bliss.) A family leaves town, and once again, Dorothy is there with her commemorative verse filled with good wishes and happy reminiscences.

These provide the only public occasions for Dorothy's literary outpourings. Her audiences are appreciative but limited. This doesn't make her unhappy. She likes doing it — and she can't help it; it's as much a part of her life as hiking through a country field.

The logical questions arise, though: *Wouldn't what you do make more sense if you were paid for it? And why go to all the trouble of writing something no one will ever read? No one is going to publish your poems; very few people will ever see or hear them. Isn't what you do just a waste of time?*

The same question could be asked of the amateur pianist. A dentist comes home from his office, sits at his piano and plays music no one except perhaps unwilling neighbors ever hears. He's not a very good pianist, and no one will ask him to give a recital. He relaxes at the keyboard and plays purely for pleasure. It would be easier to turn on the record player or radio, but he's a player, not a listener.

A printing salesman I know fills his spare time making color slide documentaries. During his holidays, he travels to the Arctic or the Mediterranean, the South Pacific or the Baltic Sea. He takes the best cameras, lenses and sound equipment he can afford. Back home, he edits his films, adapts his tapes and comes up with photo stories. He has found a happy outlet for his hobby as a guest speaker at service clubs and organization banquets. His reward may be a $5 beer mug. No matter. Others make a career of producing travelogues; he does it for fun, and his compensation in the long run may be greater than theirs.

So it is with the amateur writer.

Amateur writers, with no compulsion to work, no demanding editor or agent looking over their shoulders, and no incentive but pleasure, can experiment with style, play with words, trifle with plots and thoroughly enjoy themselves. Writing for fun may be as exhilarating as a set of tennis or a mountain climb. A middle-aged businessman I know is an author by night — and often, he confesses, far into the early morning. His problem is going to bed early enough to get a decent night's sleep. He likes to write short essays about the amusing characters he meets, and as he pecks away, two-fingered, at his typewriter, he manages to release some of the frustration that accumulated within him during his business hours. For him, writing is not only good fun but also an excellent catharsis.

Writing can also be shared — in which case the pleasure may be tenfold. Perhaps it's a first trip to Italy; you wake in your hotel room to an aria being sung beneath your window by a gondolier. Such a moment may never occur again; as a writer, you are determined to put it down, just as it is. You may put in in your diary, perhaps in a letter to a friend or relative back home, or in the form of an essay or a poem. However you write it, someday, someplace, you may be able to renew your pleasure by sharing it with someone else.

Or perhaps you paused in your morning stroll along the Newfoundland shore to chat with a fisherman long retired but still dreaming of days on the Grand Banks. His language, his manners, his rugged facial features and his tales of adventure give you opportunities galore for conversations at home, if you only get them all down in writing before you forget.

You don't necessarily need to go away to gather grist for your writer's mill. An afternoon at a cocktail party may produce revelations enough — if you have a good ear and a response-provoking tongue. And your story may be typewritten, handwritten, or spoken into a tape recorder and sent back home by wireless, satellite or airmail. What's important is not the mechanical means of communicating but the spirit and joy with which your thoughts and feelings are put into words.

I can hear you say, "Me? I can't write." You may not write well, according to the judgment of a literary critic or an editor or publisher. But everyone with the power of speech — and some without it — can write. You may not have the imagination of a Robert Louis Stevenson or the energy and drive of a Hemingway, but no one is without the ability to write a sentence that conveys meaning, and that's what writing is all about.

None of this is to suggest you shouldn't try to be a *good* writer and make every effort to enlarge your vocabulary and develop your own writing style. The satisfaction from any avocation comes not from a financial reward but from an improved performance. Good writing is obviously more satisfying than careless or sloppy work.

The satisfaction in writing comes from telling a story, describing a scene or passing on significant information, as well as from expressing feelings and writing from the heart. The sense of fulfillment is always enhanced when, in whatever form you choose to write, the manner of your telling includes use of the right words in the right order. As John Sheffield put it in his *Essay on Poetry*, written in 1682: "Of all the arts in which the wise excel, Nature's chief masterpiece is writing well."

Let's examine the kinds of writing you can do for the pure joy and fun of it.

POETRY

The poet's eye in a fine frenzy rolling,

Doth glance from heaven to earth, from earth to heaven,

And, as imagination bodies forth

The form of things unknown, the poet's pen

Turns them to shapes and gives to airy nothing

A local habitation and a name.

So wrote Shakespeare in *A Midsummer Night's Dream.* Writing poetry is a healthy hobby. Young children delight in it; in almost every home, the nursery rhyme is their introduction to English literature. Teenagers recite or write jingles and limericks.

Middle-aged men and women exchange messages in verse, compose ballads and romantic epics for reading at conventions, anniversaries and church gatherings. In old age, with time on their hands, amateur writers are known to behave as the two ancient kings described in James Hall Naylor's poem, "Ancient Authors."

King David and King Solomon

Led merry, merry lives

With many, many lady friends

And many, many wives.

But when old age crept over them

With many, many qualms

King Solomon wrote the Proverbs

And King David wrote the Psalms.

Poetry is indisputably the most popular exercise for amateur writers. Even those who write mainly in prose cannot resist the temptation once in a while to break into verse. It is, for one thing, good literary exercise, honing your skill with words and sharpening your style. One may write a poem in the form of a letter, a greeting card, a short or long narrative or a paean to Mother Nature. It may be about war, people, a tumble-down homestead or the moon over Jamaica. Poems are humorous or sad, heroic or tragic, five lines long or a thousand. Comic poems are particularly suitable for reading on festive occasions when the wine flows. They are also enjoyed by young children. And one businessman I know has found a practical use for the poems he writes. John Grimshaw, president of a large public relations company, spends his days in corporation boardrooms or on industrial locations. For relaxation, he writes poems. Each year, friends receive a home-made Christmas card composed of a drawing of the Grimshaws' 1840 stone house and John's version of the Christmas story in verse.

What's more, poetry can revere life itself: Joseph Rozel, now in his eighties, sincerely believes that writing poetry kept him alive. In the 1940s, Rozel was an inmate at Auschwitz. He watched his parents and thousands of fellow inmates march to the gas chambers. "If it was not for my poetry," he says, "I would never have survived." Surrounded by horror, he expected every night to be his last. Cold, hungry and frightened, he scrounged scraps of paper — torn edges of old envelopes, wrappings from food thrown into his cell — and with a stub of a pencil he wrote bits of poetry, expressing as well as he could his abiding faith in beauty and the eventual return of sanity to a mad world. "My poems were written from the soul, and while hundreds committed suicide or went almost eagerly to the gas chambers to end the horror, my poetry kept me alive."

After liberation, Rozel fled to America. He took a laboring job till he had enough money to open a snack bar. There, he spent the next twenty years of his life. When I met Rozel, he was conducting an informal lecture to a group of senior citizens. I asked him if he was able to make a living writing poetry after closing his shop. "Poems are not for money," he said, "they are for life, and I will go on writing them until I die."

DIARIES

Just as there are many kinds of poetry, there are different kinds of diaries: office diaries in which the busy businessperson records appointments; elegantly written and supposedly revealing diaries kept by presidents and prime ministers; diaries that accompany their owners in travels to far-off places; and the diaries that serve as "write for your life" literature. You can "talk" to your diary confidentially without holding anything back. If you have a problem, keeping a diary may be just what the doctor ordered.

There are other kinds of diaries, of course, and other reasons for keeping them, but the most common diary of all is the one kept by ordinary people who simply enjoy talking to themselves in print and like recording their daily lives, no matter how humdrum other people might think they are.

Whatever their purpose, diaries make one fundamental demand on their keepers. Diarists may start and stop, reserving their entries for special occasions or periods, but while they are keeping a diary, their keepers must attend to it at regular intervals. A diary cannot be successful if the diarist neglects it for weeks on end and then attempts to catch up by back-entering daily records as he or she remembers them.

Part of the problem is that entry-making usually is done late at night when one may be too tired to contemplate the day's events, let alone record them in legible handwriting. The first few days are the easiest; novelty provides the spur. Later, when entry after entry consists of a single line — "beautiful day; rain in the afternoon; had supper at home" — keeping a diary shows signs of becoming senseless.

If being too tired is your problem, try making brief notes in a separate journal or notebook, then on weekends or maybe once or twice a month, transfer and expand your notes for your diary. Be warned, however, that such a practice has its dangers. If you go on too long making notes or keep short and incomplete ones, when the time comes to make the transfer, you will have either forgotten or lost interest in what they were all about.

One solution is to drop the idea of a *daily* diary and confine your notes or entries to reports or comments on events or people of some significance. You might write in your diary only two or three times a month, or you might restrict it to a period of special interest: attending a seminar, taking a trip abroad, buying a home or working on a home-improvement project. Some people keep journals that contain references to only one particular interest or theme. An ardent gardener, for instance, might devote his or her diary to seasonal entries relating to catalog browsing, seed selection, ground cultivating, planting, and harvesting, with descriptions of visits to famous gardens, experiences of friends and neighbors, and talks with a horticulturist.

Commercially printed diaries have probably done more than anything else to discourage diary writing. Records of interesting occasions, worthy almost of a short essay, are restricted to so many lines under a specific date; on those inevitable days when there is nothing of interest to record, blank spaces separate the entries until the pages resemble a smile with missing teeth. Use a notebook or an ordinary school exercise book for your diary.

Diaries are supposed to be the most private of all writing. Expensive leatherbound diaries come equipped with metal locks and little keys. Within their pages is a secret world of romance where their owners may confide their innermost thoughts, however silly, wicked or selfish, without danger of discovery. The lock and key permit honest self-expression, guarding a place where you may declare who you are and what you believe. A diary should be fun to read, even if you are the only reader. Oscar Wilde, in *The Importance of Being Earnest*, had his witty hero say: "I never travel without my diary. One should always have something sensational to read on the train." There's nothing better than a literary glance at your foolish and exciting past to wile away an hour or two.

A good diary cannot be a slipshod affair. Prepare to do some honest reporting. Write in a style that reflects your personality and your knowledge. A diary is one friend you can never deceive or pass off with clumsily created drivel. Above all, save yourself—and those who may uncover your secret journal after you have departed—from reading hundreds of words signifying nothing.

LETTERS

Letter writing offers a means of expressing yourself for reasons other than self-indulgence. The novelist may put a year or more into his or her work and never find a reader. The letter writer maintains amateur status while gaining at least one and maybe a half dozen or more readers right away.

Good letter writers are rare and should be cherished by all who receive their epistles. Few tributes to a personal relationship are greater than the comment, "So-and-so writes such wonderful letters, I can't wait to receive them." A prime virtue of letter-writing is that it is undertaken with the hope that it will give as much pleasure to the recipient as to the sender.

Most people, unfortunately, don't write *real* letters—letters that communicate, that pass along news and information about their activities and interests, and that contain a sense of warmth, love and understanding. They write thank-you notes or holiday greetings, or they dictate business letters full of *whereases* and *wherefores*. Many who do write letters do so under compulsion, which shows in the end product. A parent demands a letter a week or a month from a son or daughter away at school, or one must write Aunt Nancy because she lives all alone and has no one to talk to. There may be some love or affection in such letters, but no love of writing.

Letter writing is not something to be dismissed with a shrug. It's good practice, serves a useful and often kindly purpose, and teaches you to apply your skills to a creative project. You may improve your letter writing by training your observation facilities, making notes of something you have seen or done, or of someone you have talked to, and referring to your notes when you start to write.

Organize each letter before you begin. Before launching into a letter, my wife roughs out a draft, putting down what she wants to say in reply to her correspondent's last letter. Then she lists the new information. She likes to include newspaper clippings and snapshots, and she sometimes suggests that the latter be returned so they won't clutter up the recipient's desk. By the time she is ready to write, she is well organized, and someone is going to receive an interesting and readable letter.

She has one weakness; she refuses to keep copies. Keep a carbon of every letter you write, or you will inevitably forget what you said last time and relate the same story all over again.

As with all writing, the more letters you write, the better you'll be at it. Those who must "find time to write a letter" usually don't write at all. Find a comfortable corner where you can write without being disturbed. Stake out a claim to it and occupy it at regular hours. Be sure you have paper, pens or pencils, envelopes, stamps, address books and a clear writing surface. I don't mention a typewriter; although I type all my letters, I still think handwritten ones are best — they offer something personal, warm and inviting.

STORIES FOR CHILDREN

Hickory, dickory dock,

The mouse ran up the clock;

The clock struck one,

The mouse ran down;

Hickory, dickory dock.

Whoever wrote that bit of sing-song verse several hundred years ago probably never dreamed that it would survive to amuse twentieth-century children. Yet here it is.

The most common form of storytelling is still the bedtime recitation of adventures created by even the most unliterary parents. Some are updated versions of stories they learned from *their* parents or grandparents. Others are made up on the spur of the moment, perhaps to meet a specific need.

Preschool children are willing to believe almost anything. It may be sad, beautiful or funny, true-to-life or pure fantasy. They won't question the most outrageous statements, and they find nothing unacceptable in animals who talk like people, trees that prance up and down the garden, and boys and girls who are smarter than their parents. They know what they like, and they usually ask for it over and over again: "Tell me the story about the frog who fell into the well and was rescued by the friendly goldfish."

Some of our best-loved classics by well-known authors originated as stories these people created for children in their own families. E.B. White developed the adventures of his diminutive hero Stuart over a period of years to entertain his eighteen nieces and nephews. Some seven years later, he showed the tales to an editor—who rejected them. Eight years later, after considerable addition and revision, they became *Stuart Little* (HarperCollins Children's Books). A.A. Milne immortalized Winnie the Pooh, Piglet and other stuffed animals belonging to his son Christopher Robin Milne. And a Cambridge mathematics professor, Dr. Charles Lutwidge Dodgson, wrote fantasies to entertain the daughters of a friend. Thinking such writing might be considered much too silly for a man in his position, he wrote *Alice's Adventures in Wonderland* and *Through the Looking Glass* under the pen name Lewis Carroll.

You can gain great satisfaction from dreaming up your stories, perfecting them and preserving them in writing. Such projects are much more rewarding and can have more far-reaching results than most people realize. Because the writer knows the background, personality and development of the individual child, he or she can tailor a story to fit the child's situation, interests and activities. The main character may in fact be the child for whom the story is written, or perhaps the child's pet. Privileged information may be incorporated, and a special lifelong relationship, increasingly precious to both storyteller and child, often results.

What kinds of stories are most likely to succeed? Preschoolers to children seven or eight years old welcome fantasies and realistic stories, absurd and zany stories, and happy stories about familiar events like birthday parties, picnics and visits to the zoo or playground. Favorite holidays like Christmas, Thanksgiving and Halloween always suggest good ideas. Animal stories may be about a bear with blue overalls and a stocking cap who has amusing adventures at the shopping center, or they may be about more realistic creatures like the toad who lives in an overturned flowerpot in the vegetable garden.

Little children enjoy fables about how the chipmunk got its stripes. They love any story that makes them feel smarter than the main character, for example, a mouse who thinks it's well hidden because only its long tail shows.

Start planning stories for children with a specific child in mind. True stories about how the child got his name, the circumstances and events related to his birth or adoption, and other special events are tales every kid loves to hear again and again, and they help build a sense of identity and personal worth. Recounting happy times such as a vacation trip to visit grandparents or acquiring a new pet help children appreciate these events even more.

Story writers often start out as story*tellers*, sometimes developing the tale as they go along. It's fun in situations like this to include the child or children in the creative process, though you have to be quick or your audience may not only follow you but also overtake you.

"It was a very dark night, and all the animals in the jungle were asleep," you begin.

"Except Barney the Bat," the child says. "Bats sleep in the daytime and fly around at night."

Barney may give you something to reckon with. He wasn't in *your* story at all. But there he is now, and who knows — he may end up as the main character.

But the story, no matter how fantastic, must be *logical*. Theodor Geisel, better known as Dr. Seuss, says: "I don't try to kid kids. Even fantasy has got to have logic or they won't buy it. They're so sharp that if you begin to cheat the slightest bit — for instance, if you are depicting a simply greedy man and suddenly change him into a mean man — they detect it immediately." He also warns against talking down to children: "Kids can understand any idea you are intelligent enough to state clearly. And they are ready to laugh; so when something appeals to them, you can make up any silly thing and they will go along with you. You can be as crazy as you want to be as long as you remain logical." Use simple words and short sentences with lots of action and a minimum of description. Paint word pictures by using specific details: not just "some ice cream," but "strawberry ice cream piled high in a pink cone." Stories for young children will be told or read to them, so read your story aloud over and over again and *listen* for cadence, tempo and emphasis.

Your story should be just as short as you can make it and still tell the story. Children's attention spans are very short. Magazines for preschoolers generally specify 200 to about 400 words, some as many as 600. For children five to eight, 900 to 1,000 words is the limit.

After you've finished telling your story and done what every playwright dreads — put your audience to sleep — write it all down, just as you told it. Instead of writing for some publisher, consider those of your listeners who will grow up to be storytellers of tomorrow.

It's much harder for novices to find a receptive audience among older children. By the age of seven or eight, kids have outgrown the bedtime story. They're beginning to read for themselves, and normally they have a good choice of magazines and books from the school or public library.

A few other possibilities are worth considering, however, in the nonfiction field. Perhaps you know a simple way to teach a child to tell time, or to make a bird feeder or some other object of interest to children. Maybe you have some ideas for planning and decorating a child's room for very little money — or for giving an unusual party. Or maybe you're a genius at explaining principles of mathematics or science in a simple way that makes difficult concepts understandable and interesting to kids.

Have you known someone you'd really like your children or grandchildren or others to know? One woman I know, for example, felt sad that her grandchildren would grow up knowing very little about their father, who was killed in Vietnam. So she wrote a book about him — things he said and did as a little boy, his growing-up years, accounts of his Boy Scout activities, his fishing trips with his dad, his hobbies and sports — whatever could make him "come alive" for his children. She included snapshots and photographs wherever possible. But such a project need not be limited to persons who have died or for some reason are not living with the family. After all, nobody's view of another person is the same as someone else's. A mother's or father's knowledge of a person is certainly different from that of the person's wife or sister. A "family portrait" or "family history" is another of the labors of love that any amateur writer can provide for the children of the family.

Speaking of which . . .

FAMILY HISTORIES

Henry Buzzell is a fortunate man. When he decided to become a family historian, his name made his job much easier. Had it been Smith or Jones, he might never even have tried.

Buzzell is a retired engineer. After forty-odd years with an international engineering company, he signed up for his pension. Engineering, drafting and board meetings were out. He was free to do just as he pleased — and one of the first things he pleased was to draw a bead on the Buzzell family and compile a history of the North American branch.

Buzzell personally interviewed relatives near his home and conducted written interviews with those living farther away. He gathered from available family resources what written records there were: birth, marriage and death certificates; announcements of appointments and anniversaries; copies of contracts, real estate transactions and probated wills — the usual kinds of papers one finds in safety-deposit boxes and home filing cabinets. He also asked relatives to add to their vital statistics any anecdotes or reminiscences about their family connections. Luckily, an earlier Buzzell apparently had had the same idea and had left a partly finished family record covering the very early days.

Gathering material for his history took about two years. When his manuscript was completed, he mimeographed copies and put them in loose-leaf binders. He distributed copies of the book to cooperating family members, who simply paid their share of the material costs. One copy was deposited with the Library of Congress in Washington and one with the National Library of Canada. Libraries in communities where Buzzell lived were also given copies.

The "Buzzell Family History" is not likely to hit the newsstands or to be reviewed in the *Times Book Review*. Actually, it is not really a history at all, in the sense that a history is a continuing *story* of a time and place. It's more like a blueprint — locating people and places, listing offspring and occupations. For members of the family, it remains a thoughtful and fascinating document. For Buzzell, the research, the organizing and the writing were pure pleasure and the perfect transition from an active professional life to a slower, yet enterprising and productive, retirement. He never expected to be paid for it — and never will be. William J. Hoffman, author of *Life Writing* (St. Martin's Press), thinks Buzzell was quite right. "For every writer of family histories," he says, "there is a large, sympathetic and highly receptive audience of family and friends. For many writers, perhaps most, this is enough."

Family histories may produce some remarkable discoveries for the amateur writer and researcher. Just undertaking such a project, even if it's never completed, may lead to renewals of long-neglected family relationships and introductions to interesting and congenial family members you never even knew existed. You could be surprised to learn how widely a single family may disperse in only one or two generations.

HAPPY ENDINGS

If you have an urge to tell a story, to describe a scene or a happening, to explain how to do something, or to express and even propagandize an original idea, you are a potential writer. To develop and finally realize that potential will demand practice — writing over and over again what you want to say, comparing what you write today with what you wrote yesterday and determining to do even better tomorrow. But first of all, you must begin. You want to write; go ahead and do it!

Many homes are decorated with the paintings and drawings of amateurs. Some are minor works of art, worthy of space in a gallery and potentially salable. Most, however, will remain in the homes of their creators.

Among the many thousands of such paintings in America, those of a Sunday painter were discovered and now hang in important galleries and museums around the world. That artist was Grandma Moses. She painted because she had to; her brush recreated the world as she saw it. Her primitives were the products of her own sense of brightness and gaiety and enthusiasm.

You may never create a masterpiece, never win a Pulitzer Prize — you may never even be discovered by a small-town publisher. But, like Grandma Moses, you may be an "artist" just the same — you will have made use of the gift of creativity that no creature other than the human being enjoys. You will have put your thoughts, your experiences or your dreams on paper where someone else sometime may read them. That's writing! Whatever publishers, editors or critics — or the man or woman next door — may say, you're a writer.

Never forget it.

You're Never Too Young to Be a Published Writer

Ludmilla Alexander

You may not be old enough to own a driver's license, or vote in an election, or even to have gone on a first date. But you are definitely old enough to be a published author.

Age is no factor in receiving a byline. Ability is. Editors from all over the United States have purchased articles, poems and stories from youngsters sixteen years old and under.

Impossible, you say, after seeing your highly praised story rejected nine times. Then ask Cynthia Hanson of Maple Glen, Pennsylvania. Cynthia began writing for *Seventeen* magazine when she was fifteen. She had been reading the magazine since age twelve and believed she could write as well as any of the authors who were being published. She submitted an article about her vacation with her friends. *Seventeen* bought it. She then submitted book reviews, an article on learning to drive, and a gift-ideas guide — all were accepted.

Sound easy? It's not always so. Karen Frayne of San Jose, California, had been writing since the first grade. She won poetry and speech-writing contests. Her teachers were amazed at her imagination and skill in writing. When she was in the seventh grade, she decided to try publishing her work. "I would get letters from editors praising my work, yet no sales," she said. "Some editors would jot, 'I hope you keep writing.' Based on this encouragement, I did keep writing. I ignored the rejection slips, figuring that I just got started."

Finally, Karen began making headway. One of her poems was published in "Dynamite," a section of the *San Jose Mercury News*. Then, a 270-word, true-life experience was printed in the *National Zoo Magazine*'s section for children. That piece brought her $27.50.

Cheryl Dragel of Downers Grove, Illinois, has also fought an uphill battle. She sent in two poems to *Seventeen*, and one was accepted. Success! But then, Cheryl sent in forty more poems and *all* were rejected. Did she give up? No. "I was determined to succeed," she said. "I felt that if I sold one poem then why not another? And if I didn't keep on submitting them, I would never know if I could ever succeed."

Finally, "Rain Dance" was published, and Cheryl began expanding her markets. *'Teen Magazine* and *Hanging Loose* accepted her work. When her family visited Cape Cod, she wrote about their experiences. Her article was published in the *Cape Cod Times*.

JUST FOR KIDS

When writing for *Cape Cod Times* and *Southwest*, Cheryl had to compete with adult writers for the editors' attention. And it's true that most juvenile and young-adult magazines are written by adult freelancers with many years of experience in the field. If you look closely at the magazines and newspapers that are in your home, however, you will find that many have special sections for young writers.

Other magazines, such as *Stone Soup*, actually *need* manuscripts from young authors. *Stone Soup* publishes fiction, poems, songs and drawings exclusively by children thirteen years of age and under.

What should you write about? Good question! Writers of all ages have been battling with this question for centuries. It's too simple to say, "Write what you know." Hundreds of manuscripts about vacations cross editors' desks, for instance. The subject has been written to death — and yet, Cynthia Hanson's article about traveling with friends was published. And so was Cheryl Dragel's, on her experiences on Cape Cod with her family.

What made the difference?

"I wait until I experience something before I write about it," explained Cynthia Hanson. "A long time ago, a title popped into my head about being a lifeguard. Yet, I didn't start writing the article until I experienced being a lifeguard last summer."

"We seldom receive hackneyed stories about the death of pets," said William Rubel, coeditor of *Stone Soup*. "The subject moves the young authors, and they write deeply about the death or the loss of their pet."

Rubel suggested keeping a notebook for writing — as an artist keeps a sketch pad. Authors should formulate ideas — what types of color they like and why. What they think of the morning lights, the light at dusk. What do their friends like? How do people treat one another?

Here are some more tips and rules from editors that will help you be a better — and perhaps a published — writer.

One: Get Those Nouns and Verbs Tucked Firmly in Your Brain

Editors complain again and again about the poor grammar in manuscripts.

"Often, grammar is so bad that it takes too much time to correct the manuscript," said one. Another added, "Long, wordy stories with no angle, little thought, and hardly any attention to writing style are rejected."

Two: Go for the Unique

Editors, it seems, receive the same old stuff again and again. "Most articles are rejected because they're too common or too normal to be interesting to our readers," said a *Tiger Beat* editor.

William Rubel added, "The most common problem of rejected manuscripts is formula writing. Martians are always green. Aliens always destroy the world. Poets always concentrate on winter, spring and Easter."

How many times have you read about a dog that saves a family from a fire? Or a boy who plays sports poorly but makes the winning point in a championship game? Or a girl who loses her boyfriend to a beautiful but sneaky classmate, then wins him back because she is sweet, kind and honest?

Other topics editors don't want to see are jogging, babysitting techniques and pet care.

They don't want to see such manuscripts unless — and this is a big *unless* — you can come up with something unique about the subject. Perhaps there is a twist in the plot, and the dog, after saving the family, discovers who set fire to the house. Or, perhaps the babysitting techniques are given by a teenager who has set up a business with all her friends, and they donate portions of their earnings to the company for advertising, training and self-protection measures. Then the editors may just sit up and take notice.

On the other hand, you can turn even common subjects and plots into works of art with strong writing.

For example, rain. Common. Nothing exciting. But if you write imaginatively, as Cheryl Dragel did in an issue of *Seventeen*, rain takes on a completely new dimension. Here's what she wrote:

Gingerbread people, who melt when they get wet,

take refuge under awnings and umbrellas

as the first droplets of rain hit the pavement.

I run out (minus umbrella) in bare feet

splashing in a newborn puddle

to watch raindrops dancing

on a once grimy street.

Three: Find a Gentle Critic

People who read a lot know instinctively whether a manuscript is good or not. These people can tell you if the manuscript is ready to make the rounds or if it needs more work.

Find such a critic. He may be a parent, a teacher, an older brother or sister, or even a friend. Take your critic's advice cheerfully, and follow it.

Be careful that your critics don't start rewriting your manucript to suit their standards, however. "We reject material that leaves us with the suspicion that the author had a lot of parent help on the piece," said one editor.

"Too much encouragement can be discouraging," added William Rubel. "After all, not everything is good. Children are realistic and can appraise their own work. Parents should be supportive, but not make a big production."

Four: Be Persistent

"Teenagers who have made it with *Seventeen* have been persistent writers," said one fiction/teen-features editor. "They started with a few prose pieces and poems, and kept on submitting. Then they went on to longer pieces. Finally, we turned to them and assigned material such as book reviews."

Anne Irwin of Whitefish Bay, Wisconsin, reached the envied status of having a *Seventeen* editor call *her*. With her first article, she included a cover letter, telling what she did in school, her activities, and the fact that she was in the Gifted Student Writers' Program. The editors rejected the article but liked her style. They asked her to write about teen writing; her work was published in the column "Frankly Speaking."

She then wrote about a trip to Austria with the school band and orchestra. After accepting the story, the editors contacted her to write an article about Shakespeare. *Seventeen* also sends her a list of articles that they are looking for.

Five: Develop a Thick Skin

Rejections hurt, whether you are thirteen and have been writing for a year, or forty-three and have been writing for twenty. When that rejection slip appears in the mailbox, don't think, "I'm no good," but rather, "My manuscript didn't fit in."

"There are many reasons for rejection," said one editor. "Very possibly, something similar was used recently."

"You can't worry whether your work is rejected or accepted," advised Reid Ackley, from Franconia, New Hampshire. "I sold three poems to *Seventeen*, and now I hesitate to try again. And yet, if I did it once, I should be able to do it again."

"My advice is to believe in yourself and keep trying," added Cheryl Dragel. "You'll never know until you try."

Finally, should you tell the editor your age? That is probably the most common question asked by young writers. Many editors don't want to know your age. They are interested in high-quality material regardless of the author's age. Period.

So, don't envy that nineteen-year-old just because he can drive a car and you can't. Believe me, getting a driver's license isn't nearly as exciting as getting a published byline.

The Writing Life Begins at Forty

Marshall J. Cook

A woman arrives at her first writing workshop, sets aside her walker and announces, "Now I'm going to do what I want to do."

"At the age of ninety-one, she had finally given herself permission to write," says her teacher, Lenore Coberly. Coberly was coeditor of *Heartland Journal*, a national magazine that publishes fiction and poetry by writers over sixty.

That student is not alone in having put off writing until later in life. Many of our finest and most successful writers did a lot of living before they started writing about it. Prolific novelist-historian James Michener had a varied career that included acting and teaching before he turned his talents to writing. His first success, *Tales of the South Pacific*, won him the Pulitzer Prize at the age of forty-one — surely not old, but old enough to disqualify him as a child phenom in the publishing world. That was forty years ago. Michener has been producing mega-bestsellers ever since.

A kids' doctor named Benjamin Spock didn't decide to put some of his theories and observations on paper until he was forty-three. His *Baby and Child Care* (Pocket Books) became the bestselling how-to book in America and launched the paperback revolution.

For Barbara Tuchman, writing bestselling histories was a second career. She was fifty when she published — and won the Pulitzer Prize for — *The Guns of August* (Bantam). She has followed that triumph with critical and popular successes like *A Distant Mirror: The Calamitous Fourteenth Century* (Knopf) and *The March of Folly* (Ballantine Trade).

Norman MacLean retired from a distinguished career as a professor of English at the University of Chicago before writing his first book. He was seventy-three when *A River Runs Through It* (University of

Chicago Press) was published. I'm glad he waited. *River* is one of the best works of fiction I've ever read.

And then there's George Burns. He was several hundred years old, at least, when he launched two new creative careers, as writer and as country and western singer.

"A common pattern is for a person's creativity to really take off as they reach their forties and fifties," says University of Wisconsin-Madison professor Joy Dohr. Dohr studied creativity in older adults before helping to found the Wisconsin Creative Arts Over Sixty Program and *Heartland Journal*. "Creative interests seem to become stronger with age," Dohr says.

For the writer, life truly can begin at forty — or ninety. So take heart if you're a "late starter." Far from being out of the race because of your late start, you actually bring unique advantages to your writing. Here are ten tips for using those advantages to become a better writer.

DRAW ON YOUR EXPERIENCE IN YOUR WRITING

I've taught creative writing to all age groups. My high school and college writers often ask me what they should write about. It's the one problem I really can't help them with. "Write from your experience," I say, echoing the great Hemingway. But they don't have enough experience yet.

I never get that question in my School for Seniors seminars.

You have a great pool of living to dip into for your writing. You've met scores of different people. You've *been* scores of different people. You've traveled. You've experienced life's joys and sorrows, and you've learned to recognize and deal with them when they come around again.

None of those years you spent not writing was wasted. You were living, experiencing, growing, filling the well. You were gaining insight into life, learning that situations are seldom all black or white but more often shades of gray, gaining the wisdom to accept ambiguity and to see that we are all an embrace of contradictions.

By bringing that kind of wisdom to your writing, you can create work of complexity and depth.

"They know so much," Lenore Coberly says of her writing students. "They've lived so long, and they have such a variety of things to draw on. That's what writing is," she adds. "It's what you are."

BE YOURSELF

Use your life experience to express your unique vision of the world and your insights into life. They're the greatest gifts you have to offer, the reasons editors might want to publish your work and readers might want to read it. They are gifts of self, honestly expressed.

Here again, your years give you an advantage. "You put up a lot of facades when you're young," Coberly says. "The older writer is better able to write honestly," because in your later years, "you don't care as much what people think about you."

Don't try to be another anybody. We already have an Ellen Goodman, a Garrison Keillor, an Erma Bombeck. And one of each is just the right number. Be an original. Be yourself. Lay yourself open. It's your differences that make you interesting.

"Almost all of my poems come from my own experience," says writer Cathy Stern. "We have to look into our own hearts" to discover and reveal feelings, including "the ones we don't want to own up to."

WRITE FREELY AND UNCRITICALLY

Create your rough drafts without evaluating or editing as you write. You'll capture the vitality and uniqueness of your vision.

"Something comes bubbling up from inside of me that I don't control," writer Erma Fisk says of her creative process. "It's like singing. You can train what comes out, but you can't invent it."

Writing isn't always as bubbling and spontaneous as song. In fact, if you've been putting off writing for years, getting started may be the toughest part of writing for you.

But you'll find it much easier to start a writing project — or simply to get going on your daily writing session — if you write freely, exploring possibilities, learning what you think and feel about a subject as you go, rather than trying to find The Right Way or to create The Perfect Manuscript on the first draft.

Of course, you'll have to revise your work carefully, perhaps several times. But that comes later. And when it's time to edit and refine, you'll find that your years of reading other people's words have helped to hone your critical skills.

WRITE TO PLEASE YOURSELF

There are lots of reasons to write and lots of audiences to write for. You may be trying to preserve family history and heritage for your children and grandchildren. You may be creating personal gifts for family and friends. You may be writing to influence decision-making in your community. Or you may be writing to gain fame and fortune, or at least a byline and a supplemental income. After all, it's nicer to be known for what you're doing now than for what you used to do. But whatever your reason, you must write for yourself first.

"I was writing to please myself, enjoying the re-creation of a powerful experience," Erma Fisk says of writing her first book. Only later did she concern herself with publishers and readers. "I translate what I'm seeing, what I feel, into words to make my vision real to me. . . . I have to satisfy myself before I can go public."

What others think of your writing is important, especially if you want to publish. But what you think of it is more important.

FOCUS YOUR ENERGY ON YOUR WRITING
The better able you are to bring your full powers to your writing, the better writer you'll become. And here again, you may have an advantage over the younger writer in the form of increased powers of concentration; you might have more self-discipline and a stronger sense of purpose, even of urgency, about your writing.

"My students don't have any time for fooling around," Coberly says. "They have no time to waste. Young people don't either, but they don't know it." She recalls a stroke victim who required a special apparatus to hold his arm up and allow him to grasp a pencil. Despite these physical barriers, he wrote regularly and well and submitted his work to one of Coberly's writing groups for critique.

"I want to work and work — all day, all week," admits Sondra Zeidenstein, editor of *A Wider Giving: Women Writing After Long Silence* (Chicory Blue Press). She speculates that her motivation may come from a heightened awareness of mortality, which, she says, "makes each day more intense."

"I sometimes forget to eat," Cathy Stern says. "There's a kind of concentration that's so absolute. You become so absorbed, you're unaware of your body."

Your motivation may not be that intense, but if you've recently retired or joined the ranks of the empty-nesters, you may have the additional advantage of more time — and more freedom to organize that time the way you want to. You have solitude and quiet. And you have the energy that once went into the job or the kids. Lavish that energy and attention on your writing.

If you're accustomed to the regimen and routine that a job or your children's demands may have imposed on you, you may want to establish a regular schedule for your writing. Break it into specific tasks, such as gathering information, creating rough copy, revising and researching markets, and assign time slots for each.

Unlike the world of a paying job or child-rearing, you can now develop a schedule to match your rhythms. If you're most creative at 4 A.M., or if you like to work late into the night, do your work when you're best able to do it well. If you find you're comfortable working in short spurts, with other activities sandwiching writing sessions, you can do that, too. The key is to find your own pace.

If you haven't retired or if the kids are still around, don't feel that you must wait to write. If you're ready to write, but life isn't yet ready to grant you the freedom you'd like, you must carve writing time out of each day. Write while the children are at school or after they go to bed. Write on your lunch hour. Get up half an hour earlier or skip the evening news. Claim a writing time, and once you claim it, don't relinquish it.

Work on plot lines while you mow the lawn. Tape copies of your typescript to the window above the kitchen sink, and revise while you wash dishes. Recite and rework lines of a poem in progress while you drive to an appointment. Take a copy of *Writer's Market* with you so you can do your marketing homework while you wait.

TAKE A CLASS OR JOIN A WRITING GROUP

If recent life changes, such as retirement or migration of the kids, have suddenly left you with much less human contact than you're used to, consider taking a writing class or workshop or joining a writing group for the social as well as the educational benefits.

A good writing class is a little like a good party: you'll find conversation and sharing in an atmosphere of trust. Friendships develop. Students become interested and involved in each others' lives. And the critiquing of each others' manuscripts "shares some of the elements of a good parlor game," according to Lenore Coberly.

But classes are much more than simply social events. You come primarily, after all, to learn to be a better writer. You want instruction, models, correction. And your life experience may make you better able to benefit from such instruction than are your younger classmates.

In my experience, younger writers seem to need a lot of affirmation and praise. Sometimes I almost feel that they're looking for a parent rather than a teacher. But older writers seem better able to take criticism and even to seek it out, knowing that it will make them better writers.

There are lots of exceptions, of course: serious-minded and self-confident young adults who seek and profit from criticism, older students who lack the ego-strength to hear what's wrong as well as what's right with their work. But I believe the generalization to hold true much more often than not, and I know that it's true in my own life.

When I was an undergraduate creative writing student at Stanford, I took a course from an "old man" who smiled and nodded a lot when we read our manuscripts in class, who smoked cigars and didn't talk much and wrote lengthy and mostly negative comments on my short stories. I resented the criticism and wrote my teacher off as hopelessly old and out of it. I also wrote off the guest speaker he brought in to answer our questions.

My teacher was Malcolm Cowley, the man who salvaged William Faulkner's career and edited his fiction.

His guest was John Dos Passos.

I didn't have any questions for either one of them. I had all the answers.

Can you imagine how much I'd give to be back in that classroom now, to have an opportunity to have Cowley comment on my work or to ask Cowley and Dos Passos about the craft of fiction? If you can, and if you ever blew an opportunity to learn the way I did as an arrogant undergraduate, you understand the heightened ability to benefit from instruction that you bring to a learning situation.

MARKET SMART AND PUBLISH YOUR BEST

Writing is an end in itself. Putting words on paper is an inherently healthy activity. You can process life, give it meaning and learn to accept it by writing about it. But writers like to be read, and writers who have lived and learned from experience have a great deal to share with others. Part of your satisfaction with writing may come from having others read your work. You may not feel that a work is truly finished until it has been published somewhere, and you may seek the exhilaration of testing the worth of your words against the competition.

If so, explore potential markets. Market smart, matching idea to market as or even before you write.

And know that when an editor reads and evaluates your work for possible publication, your age is irrelevant. Your years certainly don't place you at a disadvantage, but they don't give you any special privileges, either. Publication depends on the value of the material to the publication and to its readers, and on nothing else.

Know, too, that an experience doesn't necessarily have value simply because it happened to you and you've written about it clearly and truthfully. When you delve into your own experience for material, keep in mind Lenore Coberly's criteria for publication in *Heartland Journal*: "We don't publish strictly nostalgia pieces. We take stories of the past when they mean something." The writer "must make something literary out of it."

Pursue publishing vigorously, but not to the exclusion of writing new material. One of my workshop students recently submitted an essay for critique that seemed dated to me. When I asked him about the work, he admitted that he'd written it fifteen years ago and had been trying to market it off and on, mostly off, ever since. It's OK to dust off an old piece, bring it up to speed and try to find a home for it. But keep writing new material, too. That's the only way you'll grow as a writer.

Publish only your best. Poet Cathy Stern says that she has enough poems for a book and that "if I were thirty or forty I think I'd go ahead and send it off." But she doesn't yet have enough poems that truly please her. "When you're young, you can afford to put out a book where not every poem is your very best. But when you're my age, you may only get one shot. If that's going to be it, I want each one to be my very best."

SEEK NEW EXPERIENCES

When we're young, experience finds us. Change is constant. Jobs and family force us to struggle and grow. As we get older, we must keep challenging ourselves, stretching and sometimes even snapping old patterns and old assumptions, as a source of stimulation and growth and of material to write about.

DON'T COMPARE YOURSELF TO OTHER WRITERS

"Comparisons are odious," my father used to tell me, many more times than once. It's one of the many wise things he told me many more times than once. I'm only now getting old enough to understand them.

You have your own subjects and themes, your own pace, your own career. Your writing has value for you insofar as it meets your needs, fulfills your expectations and matches your goals. Your value as a writer has no meaning in relation to other writers. Sure, many got started earlier. For every James Michener, we could find a Ken Kesey, who wrote *One Flew Over the Cuckoo's Nest* while still fresh out of college. There'll always be somebody who writes more/faster/better than you do and who seems to be racking up great successes while you're plodding along.

These folks have nothing to do with you. Be patient with yourself, in terms of both the amount of work you produce and its acceptance. Measure yourself by your own abilities and goals. Comparisons to other writers are at the very least meaningless, and probably, as my father would have said, odious.

GIVE YOURSELF PERMISSION TO WRITE

Many older writers report feeling guilty when they write. "It's such a self-indulgence," one told me. "I have a hard time justifying the time."

After years of working and caring for others, writing may seem selfish, especially since it requires long hours spent alone. But far from being selfish, writing is an opportunity to share your vision, your wisdom and your experience with others.

And writing enables you to live your life more intensely. "Aging is a very exciting process," Coberly says. "The best is yet to be. We should be living life at its fullest. For me, that means writing."

If you've been putting off your writing for a long time, put it off no longer. It's never too late to begin, and you'll be in the company of some wonderful writers as you launch your writing career.

The Seven Laws of Writing

R. Jean Bryant

1. To write is an *active verb. Thinking is not writing.* Writing is words on paper.

2. *Write passionately. Everyone has loves and hates; even quiet people lead passionate lives.* Creativity follows passion.

3. *Write honestly. Risk nakedness.* Originality equals vulnerability.

4. *Write for fun, for personal value. If you don't enjoy it, why should anyone else?* Pleasure precedes profit.

5. *Write anyway. Ignore discouraging words, internal and external.* Persistence pays off.

6. *Write a lot. Use everything.* Learning comes from your own struggles with words on paper.

7. *Write out of commitment to your ideas, commitment to yourself as a writer.* Trust yourself.

II.

The Basics of Breaking In

Basic Manuscript Preparation Techniques

Candy Schulman

Throughout our childhood, parents and teachers taught us how to behave, and as adults, we continue to hear their voices inside our heads. Sit up straight, they order. Read next to a bright light, they insist. Never start the day without breakfast. . . . Don't begin a sentence with the word *well*.

Well . . . I slouch. I read in the dark so as not to wake my husband. And this morning, I ate leftover chocolate cake for breakfast. But whenever I slouch over my keyboard, I still constantly hear the voice of another taskmaster, one whom I *can't* ignore — my writing teacher. He once filled my head with so many detailed rules that I thought I'd enlisted in the army rather than a writing workshop.

Double space, his voice commands. Wide margins. . . . Replace that faded ribbon. . . . Did you enclose SASE? . . . Proofread every manuscript. . . . Hup, two, three, four.

After I made it through boot camp, however, I realized that beginning writers must adhere to certain rules in order to look professional. After all the work you've poured into them, you *should* be proud. And by following some basic guidelines, editors will treat you professionally — even if you haven't yet sold your first piece.

STAGE ONE: BE NEAT

A high school English teacher of mine used to give two separate grades on compositions: one for content, and another for neatness. Editors don't do that. I have never received a rejection letter that read, "Sorry, we can't use the enclosed article, but we're giving you an A for neatness." Yes, a handsomely presented manuscript puts the editor in a better frame of mind. The same editor might not even read a sloppy manuscript filled with typographical errors, strikeovers and spelling errors. You're competing with a slew of pros for a busy editor's attention, so you don't want him or her to think you're an amateur. Editors seek *quality*. Show them your best work in the clearest way possible.

STAGE TWO: MECHANICS

Ready for a tuneup?

If you still use a typewriter, start with a new, black ribbon and keys that are clean as the day the machine was new (use a solvent and a toothbrush or toothpick for those stubbornly clogged *e*'s and *o*'s).

If you use a word processor, as most of us now do, make sure you print manuscripts on a letter-quality or laser printer. Editors dislike reading dot-matrix; many refuse to accept them. Printers have come down in price so that almost everyone can afford a letter-quality or desktop laser (remember, too, that it could be a tax deduction). If you're caught without a high-quality printer, there are plenty of printing services that run off laser-printer copies from your floppy disks. Once again, make sure the ribbon or toner cartridge is working correctly. Replace them as soon as they fade or print inconsistently, and don't blame improper pagination or layout on your computer — machines don't make errors . . . humans do. Mastering manuscript mechanics means learning how to use your computer.

Think of your manuscript as a precious painting: You wouldn't dare leave paint splotches in the margins, would you?

Inexpensive yellow paper (copy paper) is fine for early drafts, but splurge on the best paper (white only) for your final copy. After all, this is your manuscript's debut. Paper must measure $8\frac{1}{2}'' \times 11''$, and the best choice is twenty-pound bond with a rag content. Erasable bond smudges and isn't recommended.

Let's start with the title. I prefer separate title pages, with everything centered (see the sample on the next page).

Include your telephone number, but if you live a thousand miles from the editor's dialing finger, you will most likely get your response in the mail. A word estimate in round figures (2,500 words, not 2,496) can be typed in the upper right-hand corner, although most editors can pick up a manuscript and estimate word count practically by touch.

The first page always begins halfway down, giving the editor room for notes and directions to the typesetter. Every subsequent page follows a standard format. My own blueprint is to print my last name in the left-hand corner, the page number on the right (easily set up on a

```
MANUSCRIPT MECHANICS:
    BASIC MANUSCRIPT
 PREPARATION TECHNIQUES

           By

      Candy Schulman
    777 Fictitious Street
    New York, NY 10016
```

computer using a header). Some writers include a word from their title next to their names. That word is known as the *slug*. Others place all this information in only one of the corners. The upper left-hand corner is most common, though placing the information in the upper right prevents the slug lines from being masked if something is paper-clipped to the manuscript. Which way is correct? All of them. Use whatever method suits you best — as long as you're consistent.

Jump down three double spaces and begin the text, leaving at least 1½″ margins on all sides. Computers are easily programmed to begin and end at the same point on every page. Most writers fit about twenty-five lines on a single sheet (approximately 200 to 250 words).

Double-space everything, indent five to ten spaces for each new paragraph, and indicate breaks in the manuscript with three double spaces. When you've reached your very last lively word, type *The End* on the next line. Journalists prefer using the symbol *30*, a synonym for "The End."

Short stories are presented in exactly the same manner. Poems should be typed one to a page; clip longer poems together. Poems can be single- or double-spaced.

Book manuscripts are numbered from beginning to end; don't start numbering over with each chapter. Start each new chapter halfway down the page, and use Roman numerals for chapter titles.

A few words about typefaces: Courier, measuring ten characters per inch, has become the standard. Even though I have access to hundreds of fancy fonts on my laser printer, I still submit manuscripts using this traditional typeface. It's easy to read, and editors like it. Many writers want to show off their new computer skills, but I recommend showing off your creative skills through your prose instead. You can also use proportional typefaces, such as Times Roman, but make sure you select a large enough size (twelve points).

Remember that a highly designed typeface or the use of boldface will not enhance the chances of your manuscript's sale (they may actually put an editor off). A compelling article or dramatic short story *neatly* typed on an old manual typewriter has the same chances of being accepted. But computers do allow us to correct mistakes on the screen and easily print out error-free manuscripts.

STAGE THREE: PROOFREAD UNTIL YOUR EYES WATER

Put your manuscript away for a few hours, return to it and proofread once more. If you're a terrible speller, check complicated words — even a few *un*complicated ones — in the dictionary and through computer spell checkers. Have you left anything out? Check, check and *recheck*. I often find errors on my hard copy that I may have missed under the blinking cursor.

You're allowed to make a few neat corrections on your manuscript, using standard proofreading symbols — no more than one or two to a page — but I was always too perfectionistic to allow these to mar the presentation of my words. Although I used to retype entire pages to correct one or two errors, today the writing life is as simple as pressing a key on your keyboard that says "Print."

STAGE FOUR: WRAP IT UP AND
PREPARE FOR LAUNCH

Submit one article or short story at a time. Poetry should be submitted in batches of three to six if the individual poems aren't too long. Using a paper clip (*no staples*), attach the manuscript to a piece of cardboard. A friend of mine used to steal the backs of legal pads from her lawyer husband, but you can buy inexpensive cardboards in art supply stores. I buy stationery and other supplies in bulk from a wholesaler because of a 25 percent savings. And I never have to run out in the rain for one manila envelope.

The SASE syndrome: If you want your manuscript back, enclose a self-addressed, stamped envelope (SASE). An American humorist once said, "I'd never send an SASE, because it puts a terrible suggestion in the editor's mind." Nevertheless, unless you're working on assignment, address a 9″ × 12″ envelope to yourself. Affix appropriate postage, and slide this with your manuscript into a 9½″ × 12½″ outer envelope. When mailing a query, use a #9 envelope for the SASE, which fits neatly inside the standard #10 business-size envelope.

Are cover letters necessary? Only if you have publication credits or special qualifications for writing the piece — and then enclose a *brief* letter. Avoid chatty remarks like, "I've wanted to be a writer since the age of six. . . ." Editors are business associates; share your feelings with your friends.

Cover letter or not, direct the manuscript to a specific editor's attention. If I don't have a relationship with a particular magazine editor, I pick a name from the masthead — a sensitive-sounding name. Editors in chief are extremely busy, so I opt for a senior or associate editor (many of whom are eager to discover new writers). Once an editor responds personally, I submit another manuscript quickly, with a cover letter thanking him for those thoughtful comments. Relationships develop this way, and so do assignments.

Book manuscripts should be placed loose in ream-sized typing-paper boxes. Enclose return postage and a self-addressed mailing label.

Make sure you have a copy of the final draft (don't just trust your computer's hard disk — they can, and do, crash). You may think manuscripts don't really get lost. They do — in editor's offices, and in the mail. I'll never forget the tearful woman I once saw in the post office, clutching part of her book manuscript and begging the clerk to find her missing half, while crying, "I don't have another copy!" Don't learn the hard way.

Send your manuscripts first class. Fourth class is cheaper, but slower, too. Writers need responses as quickly as possible.

STAGE FIVE: BLAST OFF!

The manuscripts you launch will often make several orbits and need to be sent back out again. Each time you resubmit a manuscript, it must look fresh. An editor wants to be the *first* prospective buyer, not the hundredth.

But manuscripts get crumpled in the mail. Editors eat your cardboards for lunch. Even though you've stamped *Do not bend* a dozen times on the SASE, you catch your mail carrier gleefully stuffing it into your tiny mailbox.

Before my first computer, I used to iron manuscripts in order to cut down on retyping. Placing each page between two blank pages, I pressed it with a warm iron (dressed, of course, in a wrinkled blouse; who had time for *that* kind of ironing?). A new title page and last page will sometimes make the manuscript look new (if the darkness of the ribbon on the two versions matches). But when the manuscript is ripped or soiled, you must retype or print it again.

Photocopies were once taboo, but today many editors accept *clean* photocopies. Check *Writer's Market* first. And what about simultaneous submissions? This is not an easy question to answer, as I've heard editors express anger about this practice, even though it has become standard among literary agents.

Some editors absolutely refuse to consider simultaneous submissions. Again, check in *Writer's Market* for guidelines. The ethical procedure is to tell the editor in a cover letter that this is a simultaneous submission. And know that you are taking a risk of alienating an editor, even though the total response time will be quicker and fairer to writers who cannot afford to wait years before each manuscript circulates.

FINAL STAGE

Put your own voices inside your head until these rules become automatic. You'll even develop a few rules and shortcuts of your own. Whenever you prepare a manuscript, make sure your final draft is perfect.

And while you're at it, sit up straight, too.

How to Write Query Letters
Maxine Rock

The three basic ways to bring writing to the attention of an editor are the query letter, the proposal and the complete manuscript. Brief, succinct telephone calls can supplement each method. Proper presentation is an art in itself, and to successfully sell what you write, you must master all three forms.

The *query letter* is the first and most basic form of submission. It is used:

1. to introduce your idea to the editor;
2. to provide a sample of your writing style;
3. to explain your writing background and your qualifications for doing the piece; and
4. to alert the editor to your availability as a writer.

The query is just that — a question — and the question obviously is "Do you want to buy a story about this subject from me?" Queries are appropriate either with an editor for whom you've never written, or with an old friend who buys your work regularly but simply needs to see it in writing before giving the idea more thought. The only way a query letter for a known editor differs from a letter to an editor you don't know is that when you're writing a query to an editor you know, you can call him "John" instead of "Mr. Smith." And you can eliminate the paragraph detailing your background and qualifications. He already knows about that.

Here's a sample query I wrote a few years ago to the editor of *Writer's Digest*. It landed an assignment for me:

Dear Bill:

"The great taboo in the South is telling. In a place where it is so important to keep the status quo, the worst thing one can do is tell. And I've told."

What did forty-five-year-old honey blonde Rosemary Daniell tell? About sex — with both men *and* women. About working with grizzled men on an oil rig and responding to their lust in that "sweaty, erotic environment." About standing over her mother's body, glad the old lady was dead at last. And about three broken marriages in what she calls the violent South.

Daniell told it all in her poetry volume, *A Sexual Tour of the Deep South*, and in a nonfiction book, *Fatal Flowers*. She's still telling it, in articles for *Playboy* and in an upcoming novel. Her reward is guilt, nightmares about being a snitch, worries when her kids read her work — and the fame and money that comes to a rising star.

Daniell is probably the hottest female writer in the South right now, and maybe the most honest. She talks freely about how hard it is to spill your guts on paper, and how necessary it is for a writer to do it. She's a fussy, deep-reaching researcher, too, and she knows how to build a convincing argument for her ideas while she's making readers gasp and giggle over her unladylike revelations.

I'd like to share those revelations with *Writer's Digest* readers with a feature on Rosemary Daniell's personality and writing career. Women writers, especially, will find that her story gives them the courage they need to fulfill the writer's duty: Tell it all, no matter how much it hurts.

I'd like to visit Daniell in her Savannah home and let her "tell it all" to me for such an article. Then, I'll write it much as I did the piece on Paul Hemphill for *Writer's Digest*. This time, I think I can get even deeper into some gut-wrenching writer's problems. And I'll come back with good photos, too.

What do you think? I'll look forward to hearing from you.

My article on Rosemary Daniell was published in *Writer's Digest*. I felt pretty sure — right from the beginning — that my query would win the editor's heart. Why? Because I told him exactly what I wanted to do and how I'd do it. I gave a specific focus to the proposed piece; I let him know I'd be writing about the particular writer's problem of telling, and the article wouldn't just be a fluff personality piece on a hotshot author. I targeted the audience, too — women writers. Writer's magazines are eager to address women's specific writing needs. I gave the editor a sample of the style I'd use in the article — words like *snitch* and *lust* and *old lady*. This was going to be an informative yet fun-to-read piece. And I promised photos to boot. What editor could resist?

The manuscript proposal serves the same various functions as a query, but it's longer and more detailed, and it usually lists your proposed research sources. *Glamour* magazine, for example, likes proposals of three to five pages, because the length serves to make the author's intent "crystal clear." And, if you can't come across with a solid explanation of your proposed article or story in three to five pages, the editor *knows* you won't be able to deliver it later.

Proposals start with a statement of purpose, such as, "This article will explore the way author Rosemary Daniell overcomes that particular form of writer's block plaguing many females: 'telling it all.' " After one or two paragraphs of explanation, tell the editor why you want to write the story (it hasn't been done before, it will benefit his particular readers, etc.) and how you intend to accomplish the task (how many interviews, talking to the subject's friends and family, historical research, etc.). You might want to include a sample opening to the article—not just the lead, but also the following paragraphs—to clearly demonstrate your style and ability to write. If appropriate, include a list of about four research sources, such as experts in a particular field, and be sure to let the editor know these sources are readily available to you. If you plan to include photos, maps, charts or graphs, tell the editor. Also, add at least a paragraph of background material on yourself and your specific qualifications for getting the job done right. Along the way, you might also want to suggest a suitable length for the proposed piece, plus a possible deadline date. (You can include such information in a query letter, too.)

The entire proposal is not a mini-article, but a solid outline of intent and an explanation of how the job will be done. Double-space your work and make sure those are neat, good-looking pages; your proposal, like anything else you hand in to an editor, is a clear indication of your professionalism—or lack of it. (For more on constructing a proposal, see *How to Write a Book Proposal* by Michael Larsen, Writer's Digest Books.)

Submitting the *full manuscript*, in my opinion, is most suitable for short stories, novels, humor, fillers and other types of writing marked either by the uniqueness of their presentation or by their brevity. Some editors do want queries for fiction, although most will admit it's hard to grasp the essence of a short story in a business letter. It's also tough trying to write a proposal for a short story, because you're practically finished with the story itself by the time your five pages are full. A proposal is a good way to tell a book editor about your novel, however.

Writer's Market is your first source of information on which of these approaches editors prefer. At the end of each listing, *Writer's Market* notes "Query" or "Send complete ms." The editors usually mean what they say.

Phone calls alone almost never work as a way to present fiction or nonfiction ideas. Editors are visual people; they want to see something in *writing*. Also, it's important for them to get a glimpse of your style on paper before they commit to an assignment. So, unless you do business regularly with an editor and sales can be clinched with a few words over the phone, you'll be asked to write a query letter, proposal or outline of some sort. The phone call should thus be used sparingly, as a guide to the preparation of your written proposal.

Submitting the full manuscript is your only choice in the case of fiction, humor and fillers, as mentioned earlier; but the best way to save yourself time, and to make sure you get your article slanted to a particular editor's needs, is to use the query or proposal. Good luck!

Five Steps to Getting Published, Guaranteed

Gary Provost

If your stories and articles are being spurned and your books are being blackballed, it's not because editors are too stupid to recognize your greatness. And it's not because other writers keep beating you to the punch with story ideas. And it's not because some editorial assistant is so jealous of your talent that he refuses to pass your work on to the editor.

It's because your writing is not good enough.

And why should it be? Have you spent as much time at the type-writer as Larry Bird has at the foul line? Have you read as many books about writing as your attorney has read about the law? Probably not. Yet, writing well enough to be published consistently requires as much expertise as any other profession.

Most people don't understand this, because almost everybody can do a little bit of writing, while nobody can do a little bit of brain surgery, for example. A lot of people can write a clever postcard from camp or a cute poem on Valentine's Day, thus forging the illusion that professional writing skills are accessible to just about anybody who wants to put in a little more effort and a few more hours. But writing fiction or nonfiction for publication doesn't require a little more effort and a few more hours. It requires a lot more effort. It requires your life. It requires you to, as Red Smith once said, "sit down at the typewriter and open a vein."

If you haven't committed yourself to learning the craft of writing with as much intensity as you would apply to any other professional field, it's not at all surprising that you haven't been published.

Published. That word, more than any other, embraces what unpublished writers dream about. Let's face it: For every writer who goes around asking "How can I write better?" two dozen ask, "How can I get published?"

How can you get published? The answer is simple, but putting the answer to use isn't. Do just five things, and I guarantee that you will get your fiction and nonfiction published consistently. Neglect any one of them, however, and this guarantee is null and void in all fifty states and Canada. Incidentally, I didn't find these five things etched on the underside of a magic stone. I learned them through twenty years of writing successes and writing failures.

1. LEARN TO WRITE WELL

If you are an unpublished writer, perhaps you have been sailing along on the convenient belief that writing well is easy and getting published is difficult. If manuscripts you think are good get the cold shoulder, that's a perfectly reasonable conclusion. But it's wrong. Getting published is easy. Writing well is what's hard.

Or perhaps you're thinking that "Learn to write well" is fabulous advice for other unpublished writers but doesn't apply to your particular situation because you, after all, are already writing well. You ought to know; you wrote it.

That's another reasonable conclusion. The trouble is that I made that same reasonable conclusion about seven books that are stacked in my closet right now under an eighth-inch of dust. The books have three things in common: Each went to at least thirty publishers; each was turned down; each is poorly written. I thought they were wonderful when I wrote them, and now I know they are awful. If you are getting rejected regularly, I can promise you that the pages you write today will make you sick a year from today. Here's the catch, and it's the most important thing I will tell you: If you are not writing well enough to get published, you are incapable of judging the merit of your own work.

You must have humility about your work. It's the only thing that can save you. You must accept the fact that your writing is not yet good enough to be published. Don't worry about it. Every successful writer has been where you are. Just accept reality and go out and learn how to write.

Fortunately, there is more than one way.

You can learn by reading writers' magazines. Some of the writing tips I pass on to my students — things like "Say things in a positive way" and "Use conversational language" — are what I learned from

Writer's Digest when I was sixteen. The magazine didn't just supplement my education; it was my education. I never went to college, and what I learned in high school about writing wouldn't even fill this page. So, read the magazines you like every month and don't skip an article because you read "something like that" once before. Every message about good writing must be repeated dozens of times before it shows up easily in your writing.

You can learn by taking writing courses at colleges or in adult education programs. As soon as one ends, take another. I once took the same course four times.

You can learn from writers' correspondence courses. These are most valuable early in your education, less so later on.

You can learn by reading books about writing. Don't ever stop. I still read them, even though I've written four of them.

You can learn through manuscript-critique services. Try this once or twice early in your education when you are making a lot of writing mistakes. As you improve and make fewer mistakes, this will no longer be cost-effective.

You can learn to write at seminars, workshops, conferences. You can learn from reading and watching good television shows and going to good movies. (Now that I think of it, you can learn as much from bad TV shows and movies.)

And most of all, you can learn to write by writing, even if it's just a few minutes a day while the soup is heating up.

2. STUDY THE MARKET

As a writer, you are a small-business person and part of an industry. Certain laws of commerce apply to all industries, and writing is no exception. One of those laws is: Create products the customer wants to buy, not products you want to sell. That means you must read a lot to learn what is a good story idea and what is not. A good story idea has something for readers. A bad story idea usually has something only for the writer.

"How to Run a Pet Store" is a good nonfiction story idea. "Ten Tips for Buying a Dog at a Pet Store" is also a good story idea. "My Favorite Mouse," a short story about a pet-store owner who can't part with a mouse named Charlie, is a good fiction story idea. But "My Ten Years as Pet Store Owner," a collection of anecdotes and interesting stuff that happened when you were running your pet shop, is almost never a good story idea. The reader has worked somewhere for ten years, too, so why should he care about your experience? If you opened a movie theater, you wouldn't expect to make a living by showing home movies, would you?

Writing strictly from your personal experience is almost never a good idea, because for every reasonable generalization there are exceptions. James Herriot, for example, is a wonderful writer who has had great success writing collections of anecdotes and interesting stuff that happened when he was a veterinarian. But my generalization here is as valid as "You can't become rich and famous by turning letters around," even though we all know that Vanna White did exactly that.

This is not to say that you can't draw from your own life to create manuscripts. After all, it is your vein that you opened. But be sure when you write anything that you are working for the readers; that you have thought about their needs, not your own; that you have written to communicate with them, not just to express your own anger, sadness or joy. If you are writing an article, ask yourself: Will readers be smarter after they read it? Can they make what they could never make before, go where they have never been before, understand what they have never understood before? And if not, do they at least feel that they were entertained during the time they spent reading this piece? If you are writing a story or a column, ask: Have I made readers laugh? Have I touched their emotions? Have I given them something to think about?

"Study the market" also means *find out where the customers are.* If you are selling shoes, you wouldn't knock only on the doors of the ten richest families in America, because you know that everybody needs shoes. Well, if you are sending your manuscripts only to *Redbook* and *Playboy* and other top-name magazines you see on the newsstand, you are ignoring 95 percent of your potential customers.

Last week, I sold articles to *Spectator* and *Meetings and Conventions* for $1,500 each, and I would bet the whole $3,000 that there aren't two people on your street who have heard of both magazines. Most of the money earned by writers for articles and stories is being paid by magazines that most people have never heard of. There are restaurant magazines like *Bartender Magazine*, business magazines like *Corporate Monthly*, science fiction magazines like *Aboriginal Science Fiction*, and literary magazines, religious magazines, hobby magazines, sports magazines, young adult magazines, even magazines about magazines. Most of these magazines are not at your local newsstand because they are aimed at groups of people, such as button collectors, who don't all live in one town.

Imagine being a shoe salesman and having an up-to-date list of people who need several new pairs of shoes every month. Well, for the writer there is such a customer list. It's a book called *Writer's Market*, and it lists more than four thousand magazine and book publishers who are buying manuscripts. This book will tell you who is buying what, how long they would like it to be, and best of all, how much they pay. "Study the market" means get this book. Read the market listings in writers' magazines. Read a variety of magazines. Browse at newsstands.

I do that a couple of times a week. Just recently, for example, I discovered that my local magazine store has twenty-seven different wrestling magazines. Twenty-seven! If I loved wrestling, I could probably make a full-time living just writing for those magazines. Snoop around in your dentist's magazine rack. That's where I first read *Horizon*, which I later wrote for. Read newspapers, particularly the lifestyle and op-ed sections and the magazine supplements, to see what sort of material they buy from freelancers.

If you write short fiction, read the magazines that publish short stories. Send to some of the small literary magazines. Instead of buying *Writer's Market*, which covers fiction and nonfiction, get *Novel & Short Story Writer's Market*, which covers only fiction but includes hundreds of the smaller publishers of fiction. If you intend to write books, whether fiction or nonfiction, read *Publishers Weekly*, the magazine of the book publishing industry. Talk to other writers. Ask them which editors they sell to, what sort of material they sell and how much they get paid.

3. BE ASSERTIVE

Many writers fail not because they can't write but because they can't take themselves seriously as writers. They do everything they can to avoid getting published. They are afraid of criticism, so they don't show their manuscripts to anybody. They are afraid of rejection, so they don't send their stories out. They are afraid of the obligation to meet a deadline, so they don't write query letters. You can't succeed if you go through life dodging opportunity at every turn, and you won't succeed if you spend half your time apologizing for being a writer.

You must sculpt an image of yourself as a professional writer, and you must present that image to everybody you deal with.

When you write something, show it to somebody who has your trust and a solid understanding of good writing. A pro can take the criticism.

When your manuscript is ready, send it out. If it comes back, send it out again, and again. Writing is not a profession for the easily discouraged.

Get professional stationery and business cards just as you would in any other profession. I put this off for many years, and I regretted it, because after I started sending query letters out on professional stationery, my sales increased. That may surprise you, but there's really no mystery about it. The editor's first impression of you comes from your query or cover letter. That's where the trust begins, and his belief that you are a pro is part of building that trust.

When you write or speak to editors, tell them you are a writer. Not an aspiring writer, not a hopeful writer, not a would-be writer. A writer.

Call the people you need to interview. Don't tell them you're thinking of maybe writing an article that you think you might be able to sell. Be confident and direct. Tell them you are writing an article.

When you see a newspaper story that might be the germ of an idea, clip it out. Don't leave the gold there for other writers to mine.

Keep track of your business expenses for writing, and take the appropriate tax deductions.

Write every day and study the markets, as we have discussed.

4. LEARN TO SELL

Having a good product is not enough. You must be able to convince customers that you have a good product. This is salesmanship. If you want to write newspaper and magazine articles, you must learn to write query letters that are brief, enticing, professional, credible and appropriate for the market you are sending them to. Tell the editor what you have to sell, why his readers would want it and why you are the right person to write it. Tell him or her exactly what your slant on the subject will be. This is the most important element in your sales pitch. And do all that in a style that is the best possible example of your good writing.

If you want to write a nonfiction book, you must do the same thing on a larger scale. Hook the editor by convincing him that there are lots of readers for the book. Pull the editor in by explaining why *you* should write the book. Finally, land the editor with a fast-moving synopsis and a couple of sample chapters that will make him or her want to read more.

If you are writing fiction, your story is its own best salesman, but pay special attention to the beginning. An exciting and compelling first page is as good as a foot in the door. If your lead is full of background information or description, you'll be wasting your sales spiel on a customer who's snoring.

Good salesmanship also means showing the editor that you are flexible enough to work with him or her. When I told a local newspaper editor that I wanted to write an article about a zany local radio personality, he told me he wanted an article about three zany local radio personalities, including mine. I said OK and got the assignment. When I offered to write an article for a national magazine about how a small city attracts conventions, my editor wanted a piece about how a big city attracts conventions. I said fine. I got the assignment. If you were selling cars, you'd be delighted to install air conditioning or a stereo if that's what the customer wanted. There is no reason you should treat your writing customers with any less consideration.

5. DEVELOP GOOD WORK HABITS

Editors are not looking for artistic geniuses. They are looking for competent, reliable people who can do the job thoroughly, accurately and on time. Professionalism in writing will open doors as fast as quality will, and it will keep them open longer.

Good work habits for the writer are largely the same as good work habits for any professional.

You present your work in the neatest possible manner. This means clean type, dark ribbons, plenty of white space, neat margins and high-quality paper. If you are using a word processor, it means you should have a letter-quality or near-letter-quality printer. Editors, secretaries and all the people who work at the publisher must read hundreds of pages a day. It is your responsibility to make those pages as easy on the eyes as possible.

You meet deadlines. Your editor has a series of deadlines as well. On the calendar for each issue of the magazine are dates when editorial copy is due, when advertising copy is due, when the material must be typeset, when it must go to the printer, when proofs will come in to the office, when magazines are due from the printer, when they are due to be distributed. The whole system depends on dozens of people doing what they said they would do when they said they would do it. You are one of those people, and the system doesn't leave any slack for excuses like "I haven't been inspired yet" or "My dog was sick so

I didn't get any work done last week." If you see a deadline coming at you too fast, call the editor and let him know. He can usually solve the problem if he is notified well in advance. But don't make a habit of seeking extensions. Reliability is a highly prized commodity in editorial offices, and when an editor says, "I don't want it good, I want it Thursday," he means it.

Developing good work habits also means that you make sure your quotes are correct and your research is accurate. One mistake in a magazine can inspire thousands of letters from annoyed readers. Several mistakes can cut the subscription rate substantially. Your mistakes also can put a magazine in jeopardy of a lawsuit, so be meticulous in your work. Editors cannot check the accuracy of every word you write; they have to trust you.

Call editors at the office, not at home. Always remember that the editor is an employee of a business, not a personal friend. Since you work at home, it feels like the workplace to you, but to the editor it is where he goes when his work is done.

Include a self-addressed, stamped envelope (SASE) any time you send an editor something he didn't ask to see, unless it's a Christmas card.

Send Christmas cards to your regular editors, short notes of congratulations when they are promoted, and long notes of congratulations when they change jobs, along with the reminder that you would be delighted to write for them at their new magazines.

Keep good copies of everything you mail.

Keep careful records of submissions so that you don't end up sending an editor a story he has already rejected.

SO THERE THEY ARE

Five steps to publication. No magic formula. No secrets. No God-given talent. Just five commonsense directions that have worked for me and for every successful writer. If you follow them, I promise that your stories and articles will be published. It will be unavoidable. You can start right now. Go to your typewriter. Write something, anything. Remember: You have to be a writer before you can be a published writer.

Ten Steps to the Top

Deanie Francis Mills

It had taken ten years to get there. My first trip to New York City — my first trip as a writer — passed as though I were dreaming it.

I met Anita Diamant, my agent. I spent the day with Ginjer Buchanan, the Berkley Publishing editor who'd not only bought my suspense novel *Darkroom*, but signed me to a three-book contract. "An author [whom] we feel has a great deal of promise," she called me.

I simply couldn't believe it was happening. As I stood atop the Empire State Building watching the sun set over the Hudson River, my husband, Kent, wrapped his arms around me and whispered, "I wanted you to have one day in your life when you could look out over New York City and feel like you owned it."

One contract for a first novel does not an owner of New York City make, of course. But I understood what my husband was saying: *I wanted you to have a chance to savor the dream.*

Writing novels has always been my dream, and it had been a long, lonely journey as I sat in an eighty-year-old farmhouse on an isolated ranch in western Texas, working around two young children (and assorted livestock) and collecting more than two hundred rejection slips.

Among those rejection slips in my office-bedroom are twenty nasty little notes from publishers and literary agents for my *real* first novel, *Raintracks*.

I withdrew my second novel, *Do Not Go Gentle*, from the marketplace after Tabitha King published her book *The Trap* (NAL-Dutton). My book's plotline and character so much resembled King's that I feared being considered a copycat by those same editors who'd rejected *Raintracks*. The manuscript still lies among my papers.

It was after this setback that I decided to get serious about writing and publishing, even though emotionally I felt as if I was falling down a bottomless pit. I committed myself to studying religiously my field's bestselling authors, to researching extensively, to writing until it *hurt*.

In my files from that same period is a letter from Diamant, to whom I'd sent the first three chapters of the novel I'd begun in the fervor of my commitment. The letter said in so many words that Diamant didn't believe I had the skill to pull off *Darkroom*.

I wrote it anyway. It took two years, and after another agent sat on it for eight months without showing it, I shipped it off to Diamant. Defiantly, I challenged her to "just give it a fair read."

Ten days later she had it in circulation.

It wouldn't sell for fourteen months.

I still have letters from supportive friends urging me not to quit, as well as the despairing journal entries ("I can't remember when I've been more discouraged or depressed with my writing or my life in general."). In my copy of Natalie Goldberg's *Writing Down the Bones: Freeing the Writer Within* (Shambhala Publications), I underlined this sentence so brutally my pen ripped the paper:

> We can touch the things around us we once thought ugly and see their special detail, the peeling paint and gray of shadows as they are — simply what they are: not bad, just part of the life around us — and love this life because it is ours and in the moment there is nothing better.

What's not stuffed among the letters and manuscripts are the lessons I learned in those ten years. If I'd known ahead of time what it would take to succeed, maybe it wouldn't have taken so long.

So I offer them to you: the qualities I believe you'll need to make your writing dreams come true. There are ten, one for each year of my apprenticeship.

COURAGE

Don't be deceived by the simplicity of this most important quality. It takes a certain amount of courage to do anything: to marry, to bring children into the world, to believe in God. But courage is especially necessary to the writer who would succeed: not just to wrench from her soul the words she would put on paper, but to send them out to be read by strangers. Not just once, but many times.

We are all afraid, and with good reason. Norman Mailer once said of this business: "America is a cruel soil for talent. It stunts it, blights it, uproots it or overheats it with cheap fertilizer."

I live in western Texas, however; I've seen beautiful flowers that seem to grow out of sheer rock.

You'll need courage throughout your career, first to get started, and then to stretch. I was terrified to write the third book of my contract, *Borderline*. What I had in mind to do had never been done quite that way before. Sometimes I was almost sick with anxiety over the risk.

After I'd submitted *Borderline*, my editor called and pronounced it "Wonderful! The best you've ever done." She had, in fact, stayed late at the office to finish reading it.

I no longer think a project is worthwhile unless it scares me half to death. You must write in spite of the fear, which is courage defined.

On my desk I keep this quote:

Courage is the price that Life

    exacts for granting peace,

the soul that knows it not,

    knows no release

from little things;

knows not the livid loneliness

    of fear,

nor mountain heights where

    bitter joy can hear

the sound of wings.

            — Amelia Earhart

STICK-TO-IT-IVENESS

This old-fashioned word is chock-full of wisdom. It may not be listed in the thesaurus, but you'll find its synonyms there: *tenacity, persistence, perseverance, indefatigability* — or maybe just a picture of a bulldog. Writers need this quality every bit as much as they need courage, because, like the athlete who has the pluck to enter a race, we've got to have the stamina to finish.

Danielle Steel's got it. She thought she was on a roll when her first novel was published. But her next *five* novels were all rejected. Five novels. But Steel had the stick-to-it-iveness to write that sixth book.

You get to be like Danielle Steel by wearing blinders. You go straight toward your goal; you do not look to the right or to the left. You just keep writing.

TALENT

We all have insecurities, and we all like to be *told* we're good, but the true artist is often able to keep going because she just *knows* she's got what it takes. If some crude individual attacks her and accuses her of not being talented, she will be outraged. She also will know better.

She will seek a second opinion. And a third.

But the most important opinion is the one that came before the first — yours. When you start to doubt your talent, go back through your work. Find a sentence that sings, a scene that moves you, some lyricism or rhythm or insight you'd forgotten you could produce.

You have talent; only the people with it ever get far enough to suspect they don't.

DRIVE AND SELF-DISCIPLINE

Achievers don't waste much time in la-la land fantasizing about being rich and famous. They're too busy working. Successful people are *driven*. They achieve over amazing obstacles and insurmountable odds. They succeed in spite of poverty or handicaps or setbacks or discrimination.

For the past six years, I've worked around a muscular disability that punishes me with all-over muscular pain, stiffness and exhaustion whenever I push myself too hard. On days when I am unable to sit at the computer, I work at a lap desk. So does a friend of mine with multiple sclerosis, who props herself up on pillows and balances her typewriter on her stomach. This is the nature of discipline.

Those of us who write with children around learn what Parris Afton Bonds refers to as "moment by moment." If the kid sleeps twenty minutes, you write. If you have to wait for the end of soccer practice, you revise while you wait. If all's quiet on the TV front, you write. You don't waste time fantasizing about secluded writers' colonies. In this manner, Bonds completed a 600-page historical saga with five sons underfoot.

STRONG EGO

You must have a strong sense of self to *survive* and *succeed* at writing and publishing.

From my earliest memories, I was born a mind wanderer, a dreamer, a spinner of tales. Writing was a thumbprint on my soul—different, it would seem, from anyone else's I knew.

For eight years, I freelanced articles to make money, scribbling unsold mysteries on the side. I hated it. Once I went two years without making a sale. Nothing I did seemed right. I nearly quit many times. Finally, I realized I'd been cramming a bawdy novelist's spirit into a freelancer's tightlaced corset. I made the decision to do what I'd really wanted to do; write suspense. It was the scariest decision of my professional life. I knew it could be another few years before I made a dime. But by "following my bliss," as Joseph Campbell would say, I discovered myself and grew strong.

EDUCATION

A college degree may make no difference in your success as a writer. But it *can* help support you and pay your bills during your apprenticeship in writing. Studying literary masters and writing papers that require research skills can't hurt.

Even if you don't attend college, your writing dreams will require *some* schooling along the way. That education can come in many forms: reading trade journals, analyzing *Writer's Market*, joining writers organizations, attending writing conferences, reading books on the craft and business of writing, studying books by bestselling authors in your chosen field, reading many things all the time. And, of course, by writing.

VISUALIZING

Alvin Toffler said, "You've got to think about the 'big things' while you're doing small things, so that all the small things go in the right direction."

Make a habit of visualizing your dream as already accomplished. The Apostle Paul, writing to the Hebrews in the New Testament, called it *faith*: "Now faith is the assurance of things hoped for, the evidence of things unseen."

Be specific. See your completed manuscript. See yourself signing a contract. See yourself having lunch in New York City with your agent and your editor.

Then, write down your goals. Answer these questions: *Where do I want to be a year from now? Five years from now? Ten years from now?*

There is something almost magical about making a commitment on paper.

Share your goals with someone you can count on to support you when the going gets rough.

Staring at a ten-year goal can be overwhelming, however, so carve it into manageable segments. Just as John Steinbeck knew that two pages a day would one day result in *The Grapes of Wrath*, so setting short-term goals will move you inexorably toward achieving the big one.

MENTOR

This is a tricky one. If you are as geographically isolated as I am, access to successful, published authors is limited. Still, a mentor doesn't have to be someone you've met; a mentor can be someone whose writing you truly admire. Read everything by that author, not to copy, but to learn.

Before I even started writing *Darkroom*, I dissected all the best-selling psychological thrillers, picking out elements that made them work, then went to work on my story, incorporating those elements as I went along.

COMMITMENT

Goethe said: "Whatever you can do, or dream you can, begin it. Boldness has genius, power and magic in it." I copied that quote into my journal on February 7, 1987. One week later, Anita Diamant accepted me as a client, and *Darkroom* was put on the market. Making commitments is far harder than making excuses. Yet I've found that when I make a commitment and *act*, doors open into rooms I never knew existed. People back me up, and things work out in the most unexpected ways.

WILLINGNESS TO SACRIFICE

This is the most far-reaching quality you need to make your writing dreams come true, particularly if you sacrifice a paying job to write full time. Unless your spouse makes a comfortable living, expect a rough financial life. You will be under almost constant pressure to "get a job."

In the early, grindingly broke years of my career, I tried everything to earn money with my writing: teaching writing classes, typing resumes, working for $5 per hour at the local newspaper, writing features for regional magazines, doing publicity work for companies — you name it. (On the side, I worked on novels.)

But there are sacrifices other than financial ones that must be made. Time and energy for other activities is limited. Housekeeping frequently comes to a screeching halt. Domestic tranquillity is often upset. Growing families clamor for attention. A disciplined writer learns to ration her time and to stand her ground when her family complains. In a writer's family, *everybody* has to be willing to sacrifice to realize your writing dreams.

ARE YOU THE ONE IN TEN?

I've come up with a statistic that isn't based on a single scientific thing. It's just my opinion, but in any given room of self-proclaimed writers, I believe only one in ten will see his vision realized, accomplish his goals and know that his dreams have come true.

Nearly half will never try. They believe their excuses for not writing. ("My husband won't let me," "My children interrupt me," "I can't stand rejection," "You have to have a big-time agent," etc.)

A few more will try. Once. At the first big setback or hurtful rejection letter, they'll quit.

Most of the rest will settle for second best. They'll become editors, or teachers, or newspaper reporters — when all they *really* want to do is write novels.

But one will have the courage, the ego, the drive and other qualities to continue to write, no matter what others say or do.

You know who you are. When you finish reading this, you'll write down your goals. Then you'll stretch back to visualize yourself at the top of the Empire State Building, watching the hazy summer sky turn the Hudson River to melted gold as you savor your writing dreams come true.

III.

Getting Under Way

Easy First Sales: Fillers

Louise Boggess

At a luncheon, the woman sitting beside me pointed to her overweight friend at the end of the table and remarked, "She bought a reducing machine last week for a ridiculous price."

The comment kept cropping up in my mind all during the luncheon as a possible filler. Before I arrived home several hours later, I had written in my notebook: "Substitute *figure* for *price* so statement reads, 'She bought a reducing machine last week for a ridiculous figure.'" The slight change made a salable filler.

Filler refers to a short item used to enliven the pages of a magazine. It may vary from a beautifully turned phrase to a personal experience of 500 words. Originally, the filler completed an unfinished page, but today, magazines use them to make up special sections under titles many readers recognize, such as "Life in These United States" from *Reader's Digest*.

Fillers and short features offer anyone an exceptional opportunity to write and sell. You can write and sell because the editor buys the material regardless of who wrote it — a known or an unknown writer. Also, writing fillers requires very little time. In fact, you simply work on the margins of time by jotting down items while you wait in the dentist's office or eat your lunch.

TRAVEL ALERT

Amazingly, you can earn from $100 to $300 a month by selling these short items. Furthermore, think of the satisfaction you derive from sharing some special knowledge, a bit of laughter, an interesting personality or a dramatic experience with thousands of people.

Writing fillers also appeals to the professional writer, but in a different way. In doing research for writing fiction or nonfiction, he comes across items that will sell as fillers. The money from these fillers helps with the cost of research. While he does not go looking for them, he rarely misses any, more or less, handed to him. But writing fillers offers only a sideline.

On the other hand, the beginner must learn where to look for filler ideas. In a very short time, she discovers fillers all around her. Think of fillers and short features as brief playbacks from life. The more you socialize with people, the more ideas you find. So begin your search for filler ideas by observing the world around you.

An alertness when traveling pays dividends. Look for humorous signs on marquees, in front of stores, in store windows, on panel trucks or on billboards. Small towns offer very fertile ground for this type of lookout. A sign on the highway said: "You Came You Saw Utah."

This sign appeared on a car wash: "Have Soap Will Wash." A carpet store advertised: "Our Prices Will Floor You." A car-body shop carried this one: "Scrap Metal for Sick Cars."

Signs appear in places you least expect. During a heavy California rain, the drainage systems overflowed, and water reached the doorways of many houses in a tract. One owner promptly put up this homemade sign: "For Sale Cheap This Lakeside Property." This resulted in a quick filler sale.

Actions of people, like words, make good fillers. Never wait idly in an airport or any place crowded with people, but study the actions and reactions of people. You may find a filler.

A young mother between planes at the airport handed her youngster a plastic sack filled with building blocks. He dumped the blocks made of colored sponges on the floor without a sound. This suggested an excellent hint for traveling with youngsters.

Emotional responses of people make good filler material. In an adult-education class for the foreign born, the teacher asked each person to either sing or recite his national anthem as a means of getting acquainted with each other. When the turn of a Hungarian refugee came, he refused to sing the song of his country but proudly burst into "God Bless America."

Your power of observation can lead you to other fillers. Watch for unusual hobbies of your friends and acquaintances. Notice outstanding window displays in stores. Take a picture and interview the person in charge so you can write a short explanation. Businesspersons use time-saving or labor-saving shortcuts in all types of work. Look for them. A sale awaits you at the appropriate business publication.

Observation offers only one means of finding filler and short feature material. You must also learn to listen.

No one needs a license to listen, but you can profit from what you hear. When a proud parent wants to tell you about the bright sayings of her child, listen. If a friend relates a funny sight she saw at a bus station, get every detail. Ask questions if necessary. By adding a few words here and there, you have possibly a salable anecdote.

Tune in on conversations of others while you wait in a crowd. Two secretaries discussed another person while waiting in the luncheon line. "She uses all the brains she has," one said. The other quipped, "And all she can borrow." A woman in the theater line explained to her friend how she mended the finger of her glove by using a lipstick as a darning egg.

Family and college reunions provide good listening for filler ideas. Everyone has sharpened his or her memory. You hear old sayings, puns or humorous incidents. Take along a tape recorder so that you can gather all the information. Later, you can run the tape at your leisure and check for filler material.

Many people earn a living by speaking with a humorous tongue. Listen with fillers in mind when you hear a lecturer, a luncheon speaker, a disc jockey or a stand-up comic. Don't overlook television, radio and comedy records as excellent means of fillers. (Short jokes and gags are uncopyrightable, but a long, humorous monologue could not be reused without permission.)

The trouble with listening is that you don't want to stop to write. But you need not depend on crowds exclusively, for you can find ideas even when you read.

READ EVERYTHING

Always read with pen and pad available. Biographies offer odd and intimate glimpses of famous people. Short stories, articles and books represent the author's best words. All suggest sources of well-turned phrases, clever puns or humorous statements. Poetry provides excellent imagery and figures of speech that will sell as fillers.

Most editors accept a short, direct quotation — say, up to 100 words from a copyrighted full-length book, article or short story — as not infringing on the copyright as long as you cite the source. You couldn't, however, quote a single line from a very short poem or song without getting the author's permission. For such a situation or a longer quotation from copyrighted material, you would write the publisher for permission. Some magazines that use fillers pay the originator as well as the one who submits the filler.

Books of quotations stimulate your mind to think in epigrams and quips. Often, a statement made in early Greece applies today. Form the habit of buying books — many are available in paperback — of humorous, well-known and popular quotations. The cost proves nominal when compared to what you can earn selling epigrams and quips.

If you intend to write fillers, study the magazines you wish to sell to. Often, one filler will free your subconscious to remember a similar incident. You have heard the old expression, "That's not the way I heard it." Often in reading fillers, you see the possibility of an entirely different one for another market.

Take, for instance, the book title *Happiness Is a Warm Puppy*. You can define happiness in any number of ways: Happiness means learning your neighbor's boy no longer serves as Scout bugler. Try some spinoffs yourself on defining happiness.

Newsletters and in-service publications of organizations often contain filler material. From one newsletter came this unusual fact: "The world's only international streetcar line runs between El Paso, Texas, and Ciudad Juárez, Chihuahua, Mexico."

Read annual reports for historical facts, new scientific research or new products. You may sell a scientific or unusual fact, a new use for an old product, or information on a new one. Other similar sources of fillers include sales and promotion letters, envelope stuffers and advertisements.

Study your newspaper for funny typographical errors. *Reader's Digest* printed this one from a Kentucky newspaper's society report on a New Year's Eve party: "The large room was vividly decorated with red noses." Headlines may appear funny, too. Take this one published in the magazine of the Brazil *Herald*: "Birth Control Bears Fruit."

SHORT STUFF

Regular news stories relate antics of animals, odd coincidences in unrelated events, and happenings in the lives of well-known people. Some paragraphs from the newspapers lend themselves to humorous comment, as appears in *The New Yorker* filler. You may use any news material from a newspaper, since news, like facts, is uncopyrightable. Signed feature articles and syndicated columns, however, are copyrighted, and only brief excerpts could be used (with credit to the writer or columnist) under the fair-use provision of the copyright law.

So, make any reading you do pay dividends in money as well as pleasure.

Consider your own experience the primary source of all filler material. Some editors like first-person experiences because they provide one-to-one contact with the reader.

For example, train yourself to look for fillers as you clean house, sew or cook. If you think of ways to entertain your children or to work out an agreeable solution to a family problem, you may likely have filler material. Always make notations immediately on children's funny sayings, before you forget them.

In addition, look around your office for shortcuts to better business. If you have a home shop, look for better ways of handling a task there. Farmers seek shortcuts to better farming.

More and more magazines have added fillers and short features. To expand your sales, get acquainted with *Writer's Market*, which lists many magazines that buy fillers and short features. You can locate this information easily by the specific subhead "fillers" under each listing.

When you become more experienced in searching for material, you will develop a built-in antenna that alerts you constantly to filler material.

How to Break Into Your Local Weekly Newspaper

Bim Angst

Editors at the more than 7,000 weekly newspapers in this country are crying, literally, for good local features. I know. I'm one of them, and I wail each week when I scan the personal announcements and club news sent in by my fifteen correspondents. In their own neighborhoods are stories I'd love to publish, but I don't have the time to write them myself, and I can't afford the time to train a staff writer to get the stories for me. At night I dream of discovering six freelance writers who could supply me with the local features I need every week. But I'd be satisfied with one writer who could give me six features.

I have a file cabinet full of feature ideas that I'd love to pass on to someone else. But first I want to know that person is capable of recognizing feature possibilities. If you've got the notion that everything has feature possibilities, move to east central Pennsylvania and give me a call — fast.

Developing the idea for a feature isn't nearly as easy as finding an idea. Sure, I'd love to know about the new road signs the neighboring borough of Nesquehoning just put up, but a business profile of a sign factory in Wisconsin isn't going to interest my readers. However, the story, using the words of the designer, of how he studied the topography of the town and used his impressions to design the signs — well, for that story I'd give you the run of my own office, complete with phone and typewriter, for a whole afternoon. I'd even let you borrow a photographer.

The key is local interest. I don't care what the Canadians are doing about noisy geese — unless the local town of Tamaqua is trying out the method. I don't want to read about heart transplants — unless a lady who grew up in nearby Albrightsville is recovering from one. My readers aren't concerned with the high cost of living nationwide; they want to know what ground beef costs in Lehighton. We may feel compassion for the plight of farmers in Iowa, but here we need to know who will lose his job if a farm in West Penn Township goes under.

Every story has a local angle. That's why the weekly newspaper exists. Big-city dailies give us all the news we want about the world, the nation, even our home states. But we want to know about our neighbors, too, and the weekly newspaper is trying to satisfy that desire. The feature story is the weekly's stock-in-trade. The dailies inevitably beat it to fast-breaking news, but because the staff of a daily is geared toward what happened today, the stories that take time to unfold are often overlooked. Because there are so many car accidents, drug busts, council meetings, sports scores and murder trials to report, the daily newspaper cannot hope to cover the birthday parties for ladies turning one hundred at Weatherwood (the Carbon County Home for the Aged), the efforts of the Little Schuylkill Conservation Club, or the effects of the burgeoning tourist industry on the life-long residents of Old Mauch Chunk. The weekly covers all these stories precisely because it cannot compete with the daily for fast-breaking news.

Because he's not concerned with putting out another issue in sixteen hours, the editor of a weekly newspaper may have more time to talk to you than would the editor of a daily. Get to him on the day his paper comes out. All his work was complete the day before, and he's searching hard now for people to write the features he wants to run next week. Give him a call and ask to come see him. Don't tell him you are a freelance writer. (Editors at weekly newspapers have a fear of freelancers. They think freelancers are prima donnas who insist on complete editorial control over their work and demand hundreds of dollars for each article.) Tell him you have some ideas for features and you'd like to write them for his paper. When he tells you he can't pay much, bite your tongue and tell him you understand. Then forget about the money for a bit and go sell him your ideas.

Editors at weekly newspapers are often also sales reps for the advertising their papers carry, so keep your pitch as direct and brief as his would be. The editor just wants to know enough to feel confident that you can write the story you say you can. If you've got published clips of newspaper features you've written, take them for him to peruse. If you don't have clips, don't panic. Type a brief list of questions for each of your article ideas and let him look at those.

Here's an example: Suppose your neighbor belongs to a pistol club, the Women's Pistol Club, which has a target range in Aquashicola. The club's been active for years; members have even taken championships. The sports editors of the dailies cover events and results, but no one has ever featured the women sharpshooters. Your article suggestion might look like this:

- Why do members join?
- How do their boyfriends, parents, husbands and kids handle having them shoot pistols?
- Do they feel they're encouraging violence?
- What do they get out of shooting?
- Do their size and strength affect their shooting style?
- How do they rate against men shooters?
- Do they face bias from judges and audiences? If so, how do they handle it?

It's a lot more than finding out who the coach is and how many members there are, although that background information is necessary and useful.

Here's another possibility for an article: The Chief of Obstetrics at Coaldale Hospital is retiring. Every paper will do a feature on the man, but yours will stand out — and has to because it's in a weekly and will probably hit the streets later than the stories in the dailies — if you focus it differently. Of course, you'll have to ask how many babies he's brought into the world. But then go further. Speak to several women whose children he delivered. Find a family where he delivered a daughter and then the grandchild. The family angle and contrast of birthing styles may be very interesting. It will be just as interesting if there is no difference in birthing styles over twenty to forty years. Did he deliver his own children? If no, why not? How do the nurses feel about working with him? Has he delivered any of their children? Speak to his wife and family and find out the joys and trials his profession has placed on them. If he delivered your kids, you've got a very special story in the works already.

Ask the right questions, and your editor can make the answers into a feature. If you can't ask the right questions, it won't matter how nicely you craft a sentence. When the editor says he'll look at your article but he can't promise you anything, consider yourself in like Flynn.

But don't leave his office yet. Go over your list of questions with him. Ask for advice. Is this problem of houses and trees slipping into abandoned mines, what's called *mine subsidence*, important to the people who live near the quarries in Palmerton? The editor will be glad to tell you how to get to the quarry so you can talk to the people who live near it. Would it be wise to get the county planning director to comment on the problem county-wide? Would a contractor be able to provide information on how it influences new building? The editor will be glad to give you phone numbers.

Call the people he mentions. Mention to them that he told you to call. They may be more willing to talk to you, and more informative, if they know you're working for a newspaper editor. Use your editor's suggestions as a guide for your research.

Okay, so now you've spoken to everybody you can get to in the time before your article has to be on the editor's desk. (Ask the editor what the deadline is for the upcoming issue. Don't make him wait for your story. He might forget you, or worse, might remember you're late with your piece.) Now you have to shape the information into something people will enjoy reading. People read features for pleasure. Use any method you can to organize your story into something that's pleasant to read. If you've got a good lead, the pieces of your research will fall together almost by themselves. Quotes convey the personalities of your sources and their attitudes on your topic. A light touch will keep the reader reading.

To tailor your article to the interests of the newspaper, read the features they've printed recently. How are they focused? Who are they aimed at? What are the interests of the readers? The more detailed a picture of the readers you get, the more pleasurable the article is. Play detective. Writing for your audience means a lot more than knowing that the reader lives in Summit Hill.

When you get through the first draft of your feature, it will be at least three times longer than it should be. It should be just long enough to tell the story but short enough to ensure that the editor will use it no matter how tight the paper is the night it gets pasted up. Brevity is your ticket to getting published. Editors are realists, especially when confronted with a page that has only twenty column inches for text. Take out your flowing prose, and ax the extraneous background information. Get down to a single focus. (The background you dug up was necessary: You can't recognize a good lead or strong focus if you don't have the whole picture first.)

Then think about where your newspaper is read. It will be read in spurts — while the potatoes are boiling, while the kids are in the tub, while the reader is waiting for the carpool driver to show up. If the reader scans and finds an article too long, he'll skip it. The editor will get no good comments on it, and he won't want to see another article from you next week.

After you've custom-fit your article, the editor will refit it, sometimes brutally. He'll cut whole paragraphs, rearrange points, alter headlines and reduce your prose. This is his prerogative. Remember who's paying you.

You probably won't get paid for your article before it's published. But you'll get more efficient. Console yourself for now with the knowledge that you'll use the clippings of that newspaper feature to get assignments at regional and national magazines. The feature may have provided you with the basic research for an expanded article on the same topic. That dinky feature proves you're capable of asking the right questions and focusing and shaping the answers, and that you can handle even the most drastic editing. (Even big-time editors don't want to deal with prima donnas.)

As you move on to the big time, don't forget about your weekly newspaper editor. He pays your mileage and postage. Show him you can write consistently and that you've learned quickly, and he'll start talking per-assignment rather than per-line fees. Prove to him that you can deliver what he needs when he needs it, and he'll consider giving you a press card and making you a staff writer. Show initiative and assertiveness, and he'll make you assistant editor. I would.

How to Self-Syndicate Your Newspaper Column

James Dulley

For two years, my column "Cut Your Utility Bills" appeared weekly in the *Cincinnati Post*. Like every newspaper columnist, I dreamed of being carried by a major features syndicate. But syndicates prefer to sell columns nationally, and my weekly column on energy and water savings in the home and energy-efficient construction was rejected by all the major syndicates because it lacked national appeal.

But today, my column is read by more than two million people in twenty-five newspapers. In effect, I became a minisyndicate that carries only one column — mine. Like a major features syndicate, I handle the marketing, invoicing and distribution of individual columns to each newspaper. But unlike the columnists whose work is distributed by syndicates, I share a sales commission with no one.

Self-syndication isn't complicated, but it does require a thorough and detailed marketing plan from the start. After experimenting with several methods, I've found these steps to be the most successful. They can work for you, too.

1. Select your column topic.
2. Sell your column to your local newspaper.
3. Establish your column locally.
4. Approach major metropolitan newspapers.
5. Establish your column in three to five major papers.
6. Approach smaller-circulation newspapers.
7. Establish your column in at least twenty smaller papers.
8. Approach the major metro newspapers again, or approach a major syndicate.

CREDENTIAL INSURANCE

Before you can syndicate a column, you first must establish the column and land a home-town client. The topic of your column will be a subject in which you are an expert or one in which you can easily establish your expertise. Publish articles in trade journals and become active in local chapters of the appropriate professional societies. Offer to teach continuing-education courses related to your topic at local colleges and high schools. You'll need these credentials when you approach your local newspaper editor.

You'll also need five or six sample columns. As you choose your column format, build in a means to measure reader interest. In each installment of "Cut Your Utility Bills," I offer free, do-it-yourself instructions, diagrams and other material to readers who send me a self-addressed, stamped envelope. Question-and-answer columns are also an excellent way to measure interest.

Samples and credentials in hand, arrange a meeting with the appropriate section editor of your local newspaper. Also present samples of your other writing, a resume and professional references. Treat this meeting as a job interview, and be prepared to wait several weeks for the editor's decision.

From the start, write and handle your local column as if it were already being distributed to other newspapers. Most newspapers prefer a once-a-week column in the 500- to 600-word range. Include related sketches, diagrams or charts as needed. (Most papers have an art department that can rework your sketches, so a rough sketch is often adequate.) I mail packets of columns, with an invoice, to my editor at the beginning of each month. I date each column for the week that it should appear. If the paper skips the column for a week, the newspaper is still billed.

Also arrange to have the mail generated by your column sent in care of the newspaper instead of directly to you. I've found that more readers respond to this system — plus, the newspaper editors can see the reader response. (When readers send their questions directly to me, I regularly inform the editor of the quantity.)

Plan on writing only for your local newspaper for at least one year before marketing your column to others. It takes that long to establish your column's success, the readers' interest and your reliability in meeting deadlines and responding to readers' questions. Work closely with your local editors during this initial period. Their support will help your marketing attempts, and they may provide excellent sales contacts. Someone at one newspaper always seems to know someone at another.

As you begin your self-syndication sales effort, remember that it's both unrealistic and unproductive to mail reams of samples, expecting fifty major newspapers to pick up your column. Set a goal of being carried by three to five major metro newspapers. Look on this first marketing foray as a learning experience, a time to refine your sales technique. If I had approached every newspaper as I did the first several, I'd still be writing for only the *Cincinnati Post*. During the first several months, I revised my presentation materials eight times.

Although direct sales calls are generally considered the best sales technique, it is neither feasible nor effective to travel to many prospective newspapers. A direct-mail sales approach, on the other hand, makes contacting two hundred newspapers economically feasible.

I have found that the most effective and least expensive direct-mail sales approach is the tickle/reply card method. This approach netted me an outstanding 25 percent initial response from managing editors of the target newspapers.

Your only purpose in this first mailing is to tickle an editor's interest and to find the appropriate contact at a newspaper. The direct-mail tickle/reply introduction packet consists of a short cover letter from you, a testimonial letter from the managing editor of your local newspaper, a complimentary reader letter, a reply card requesting your complete samples packet, and a self-addressed, stamped envelope. Don't send any sample columns. Simplicity is the key. The managing editor of a target newspaper should be able to read your entire packet and fill out the reply card (naming the appropriate section editor who should receive your samples) in less than a minute.

Keep in mind that you're at a disadvantage. Many newspaper editors have an aversion to buying columns from freelancers. We tend to be less reliable than major syndicates. And since we usually can't transmit our columns electronically like the wire services, someone at the newspaper will have to type the column into the paper's computer typesetting system.

To combat this predisposition against you, develop a professional-looking introduction packet. To your potential clients, that packet is you. Use typeset and printed reply cards and return envelopes. Personalize each cover letter with the editor's name and address.

Develop your mailing list using the *Editor & Publisher International Yearbook* (Editor & Publisher Co., 11 W. 19th Street, New York, New

York 10011-4234). It lists newspapers by state and city and includes a roster of each paper's major editors. Select the names of major papers — two hundred thousand circulation or larger — for your mailing list (but never query more than one paper in the same city). Include any newspaper that is associated with your home paper. The first publication that I syndicated my column to was part of the same newspaper group (Scripps-Howard) as the *Cincinnati Post*.

Address the introduction packet to the managing editor — he can refer your material to the appropriate section editor. Have a complete samples packet ready to mail to papers even before you send out the tickler packet. You can expect 70 percent of those who will respond to do so within a week, and then it's critical for you to respond quickly, while your name is still fresh in the editor's mind.

In your samples packet, include a detailed cover letter, additional testimonial and complimentary readers' letters, a description of your expertise in your column's subject, other related publication credits, a column as it appeared in your local newspaper, and five to seven sample columns in the form that the newspaper will receive them. These samples should present a broad range of topics within the subject area.

Stress the one major advantage you have over a national syndicate: You can individualize your column for each newspaper. In my column "Cut Your Utility Bills," I calculate energy savings and costs according to each area's specific utility rates. I also make allowances for seasonal differences, switching from heating-oriented columns to air-conditioning-oriented ones sooner in the Kentucky newspapers than in the Wisconsin publications. Although this personalization requires more effort, it's a major selling point for you. A word processor minimizes the time required for this task.

SUBSTANTIAL RETURNS

Don't mention specific costs in your cover letter. Simply tell the editor you'll be in touch to answer any questions and to discuss the cost.

Make your follow-up call about five days after mailing the packet. If the editor hasn't reviewed the package, call again a week later. Usually, an editor will have a price in mind that fits his budget. You can expect a starting rate of about $25 per column from a newspaper with two hundred thousand circulation. Rates vary considerably depending on region of the country and each newspaper's specific competition. Don't be disappointed if the rate the editor names is much lower than the amount you are paid by your local newspaper—a paper always pays more for locally written material. You can always raise your rate once you prove your column's success. Remember, your goal at this stage of self-syndication is to get established.

Many papers will request a four-to six-column trial period to gauge reader interest. Although I hesitated to accept this arrangement, each newspaper that ran the trial of "Cut Your Utility Bills" ended up buying it. I now offer the free trial but stipulate that if the paper later buys the column, it will be billed for the trial columns also.

Start out each new client newspaper with several columns that drew the strongest reader response in your local newspaper. Then switch over to new columns. Don't try to recycle all your previous columns.

Along with your home paper, these new clients will be the backbone of all future marketing efforts. So *satisfy their needs*. Respond promptly to readers' letters. Even add postage when they've forgotten it. You can't afford to have even one reader call the newspaper with a complaint. Also, keep in contact with your new editors, sending them copies of unusually complimentary readers' letters and telephoning about once a month to make sure they are satisfied with your work. If possible, visit these editors after they've run your column for about two months, after your column has had a chance to prove itself. This is the ideal time to request a testimonial letter from the managing editor. The letter should cover two main points—the strong level of reader interest and your reliability and professionalism. Don't be shy about saying what you would like the letter to state. If you have handled everything professionally to this point, they'll probably be more than willing to help.

Now you're ready to approach the editors of smaller-circulation newspapers. Your goal is to pick up another twenty to thirty newspapers to gain that truly syndicated status. Be selective in developing your mailing list; I chose newspapers with circulations of ten thousand to fifty thousand—small, but large enough to pay a reasonable rate.

Use the same tickle/reply, direct-mail approach as before, but now include additional testimonial letters from your new-client newspapers and readers. You will be pleased with the number of returned reply cards from this mailing—I received more than 25 percent back. Use the same samples packet as before to follow up, except you'll want to add testimonial letters and columns as they appeared in each of the major metro newspapers.

The rates paid by smaller newspapers vary more than among the larger papers. In your follow-up call, openly ask the editor what he pays for columns, and don't let your pride keep you from reaching your goal. Some very small papers pay me as little as $6 per column. But the $6 to $10 per week from each of my twenty smaller newspapers adds up.

Although the financial return on your marketing effort hasn't been exceptional to this point, you have grown, in a short time, from local freelancer to syndicated newspaper columnist. You're now at a crossroads. You can choose to approach the features syndicates, using your broad-based success as a sales tool, or you can compete with them, adding more major newspapers to your personal syndicate. Either way, you're on the road to professional and financial success.

Getting Great Ideas for Your Greeting Cards

Molly G. Wigand

Good greeting card writers can come from anywhere. This simple truth became obvious to me during my tenure as a writer and editor at Hallmark Cards. The company looked at colleges and universities. They tried ad agencies and newspapers. While they had some luck there, they also wound up hiring:

A cashier, a rock musician, an ex-nun, a drywall installer, a biologist, a secretary, an elementary schoolteacher and a psychiatric nurse.

Greeting card writers. All types of people, from all types of backgrounds, from all over the country. But they all possessed one very special talent: the ability to tap into the feelings — love, friendship, sorrow, joy — of the American consumer.

If you have that special talent, you can write and sell greeting cards. But you must know a few tricks of the trade for bringing zing, originality and brevity to your ideas.

BRAINSTORMING

The greeting card starts with an idea — and the following three steps will help you come up with salable ideas for card copy.

Know Who Your Market Is

Who will be looking at your writing? Young? Old?

Greeting card companies often publish "needs lists" that tell what kinds of cards they're looking for; these lists also contain detailed market information. Send each company a self-addressed, stamped envelope and ask for such a list. (You'll find the companies listed in *Writer's Market*, published by Writers Digest Books.)

If you can't get a list, study the cards at local gift shops. What types of cards seem popular with consumers? What cards are classics — those you remember from years ago? Stores usually put the newer stuff near the front.

Also trust your own instincts — feelings picked up from media- and people-watching. Do you see sarcastic humor being replaced by kinder, gentler cards? A return to sincerity? One way or another, determine as much as you can about your market.

For instance, who are the senders and receivers? They're probably female (more than 90 percent of card purchasers are), but what are their age range, marital status, income level? What are their likes, dislikes, hobbies, favorite TV shows?

What types of cards are needed for various situations — such as "From Mother to Daughter at Graduation"? What types of writing would be appropriate: verse, prose, humor, cute? And what sorts of designs should accompany the writing?

Empathize With Both the Buyer-Sender and the Receiver

I believe the most important attribute of a good greeting card writer is the ability to empathize. Enter the mind — and heart — of the consumer you've pictured through your research. Imagine who the receiver is through the feelings and perceptions of the sender. What does she need or want to hear? What will brighten her day, cheer her up, make her laugh?

One tip for male writers: Because the vast majority of greeting card purchasers and senders are female, write these words on a 3″ × 5″ card and tape it near your work area:

> Except when otherwise noted,
> you are a woman!

Make an Idea Sheet

While you're in your empathetic state, jot down some feelings and ideas you think the sender would want to communicate to the receiver — not actual writing, mind you, but just the raw thoughts or ideas. If you're writing a card a mother can send to her daughter for graduation, empathize with the mother. Say to yourself, "I *am* that mother. I've raised my daughter for twenty-plus years, and now she's graduating from college. What are my feelings?" And you jot down:

> Pride, proud of you, miss you, time flies, great kid, great times,

memories, future, graduation present, moving out of house, good luck, used to wear my clothes, seem more like a friend, cap and gown, diploma, grew up too fast, bursting with pride, apartment, job hunting, seems like yesterday, world is yours

Got the idea? Keep going until most of your ideas are on the page.

START WRITING

Now let's take our rough list of ideas and refine the best ones into card copy. First we'll write off the tops of our heads (which *is* an effective method), and then we'll look at exercises successful card writers use to spark their imaginations.

While in your empathy mode, look at the ideas on your idea sheet and try to say them in some kind of clever, memorable or unique way. Write down everything that comes to mind; later, you can underline your best ideas.

I'll pick a couple of ideas from our list and start building on them:

Pride/proud: I'm so proud . . . how proud am I? . . . *I'm bursting with pride* . . . what things burst? . . . balloons? . . . balloons bursting with words coming out . . . "pride" coming out? . . . bursting at the seams . . . *It seems I'm bursting at the seams* . . . *I'm so proud I can hardly contain myself* . . . proud as a peacock (forget it, peacocks are male!)

Seem more like a friend: *You've always been a terrific daughter. Over the years, you've become a terrific friend!* (Nice, but needs congrats) . . . Mom/Best Friend . . . *Congratulations from BOTH of us . . . your mom and your best friend!* (design would be only one mom-type person) . . . *As a daughter, you've been more like a friend. As a mom, I've never been more proud!*

Usually you won't be completely satisfied with the copy you've created by playing off your idea list (even if you are, better ideas may await). That's where these five tricks of the trade come in:

Play "What If?"

Let's say your idea sheet for a humorous birthday card to be sent from a woman to another woman included the word *chocolate*. Your "What if?" questions might run like this:

• What if the sender was made of chocolate?

- What if the world was made of chocolate?
- What if chocolate came in different colors?
- What if there was chocolate champagne?

Then try to turn your questions into actual copy:

If chocolate came in different colors, I'd send you a rainbow today.

They've invented the perfect birthday drink . . . chocolate champagne!

Here's the perfect birthday toast to a real chocolate lover!

Use Comparisons

The literary terms are *allegory*, *metaphor*, *simile* and others. But all we need to know here is how to hook one idea to another.

Chocolate is like life.
Chocolate is like sex.
Chocolate is better than sex.
Chocolate is eternal.
Chocolate is an ocean.

Some of these thoughts should generate ideas:

If the ocean were chocolate, I'd send you a tidal wave for your birthday!

(The letters of the word *sex* in chocolate.) Here's a birthday card that combines your two favorite pastimes!

Play With Words

Rhymes, puns and alliteration can generate ideas.

What rhymes with the words on your idea sheet? *Birthday/Mirth Day. Getting older/Getting bolder.*

Puns deserve a word to the wise: No matter how clever or how original or how inventive, puns almost always sound corny to the ear.

(See what I mean?)

When all else fails, use alliteration (words that begin with the same sound — *tiger, temptress, pterodactyl*). It's strong. It's memorable. And people just seem to like it.

Use Substitution

Let's say you're still focusing on *chocolate* from your birthday idea sheet. Think of phrases that don't have the word *chocolate* in them, but could use it as a substitute:

> Give me liberty or give me chocolate!
> A fool and his chocolate are soon parted.
> Go ahead, make my chocolate!

Obviously, these won't always make sense.

Substitution works well when you rhyme your idea words. If your idea word is *pride*, jot down statements containing its rhymes, and then substitute:

> Pride: side, wide, fried, ride.
> Go along for the *ride*.
> Go along for the *pride*.

Flip-Flop

Think opposites. What *isn't* chocolate? What *isn't* friendship? Who *don't* you love? When is a cat *not* a cat?

SENDABILITY

This section could save you thousands of hours of fruitless labor and could be worth thousands of dollars to your income.

You must check your ideas for *sendability*—maybe the single most important factor determining whether a card will sell. *Sendability* is the attribute of a card that makes it buyable and sendable: Broad sendability means many people can buy your card and send it; limited sendability means fewer can.

The broadest sendable card in the world features no design and the word, *Hi!* Why? It has no flowers to make it feminine, and no cartoon to make it humorous. It doesn't specify an event ("Happy Birthday"). You've got a card that could be sent by anyone to anyone at any time for any reason. You've also got the world's most boring greeting card; it's so sendable there's nothing to it.

People like cards that are specific and seem "just for them." A good greeting card writer walks that tightrope between "specific enough" (to give the card a strong just-for-me appeal), and "too specific" (which excludes too many potential purchasers).

Let's look at five elements that limit sendability, and the effects each has on your copy:

Tone or Style

Once you get your empathy skills working, tone and style (formal, informal, humorous, traditional, conversational, colloquial, satirical, etc.) should become instinctive. If you're comforting a friend going through a rough time, you probably won't write humor or satire. If you're teasing someone about turning forty, your writing won't be formal.

Pronouns

The important ones are *I* vs. *we* vs. no pronoun at all. Most editors like writers to keep *I*-ness and *we*-ness out of cards. This gives them a card that can be sent by either one person, a couple or a group.

Next time you're browsing a card rack, notice how many cards exclude *I* or *we*. Instead, they say things like:

Outside: Heard another birthday cake was headed your way.
Inside: Hope the candles don't set off the sprinkler system!

In either sentence, you could have had *I* or *we* starting the lines, but this way, it communicates and retains its sendability.

Of course, there are times when *I* is preferable (romantic love, conversational prose) and times when *we* is better ("We wish you a Merry Christmas!"). There are even times when you want to specify the recipient with *you both* (wedding, anniversary).

Descriptive Words

Remember, not everyone is pretty or strong or caring or funny, the kindest, most wonderful, the greatest or the best. You will use these words to pay someone a compliment. But when you use them, think about how they limit the sendability, and use the ones most broadly applicable.

Esoterica

Be cautious of slang, regional terms, intellectualisms, etc. A Texan might understand what's meant by *giving someone sugar* on Valentine's Day, but the first time I heard it (recently), I thought about the white, granulated stuff. Don't disregard all fads and trends; these can be a great resource for generating new ideas. How many people and products capitalized on the classic "Where's the beef?" campaign, or on the *E.T.* craze?

Personal Nouns

Watch who you're calling what. People call each other a lot of names, and some of these terms of endearment are more limiting than others. Note the difference in these two lines:

> Mom, you are wonderful. . . .
> You're a wonderful Ma. . . .

GET YOUR GREETINGS OUT

You should now have pages of phrases and ideas. Keep them to yourself (for a while).

What you submit to greeting card publishers should be only the catchiest and most original of all your ideas.

You'll also need to make sure your submissions go to the proper places. The main thing to remember is always to send for — and study — each company's guidelines.

Also remember never to underestimate the importance of your task. Even the most humorous of greeting cards is bought because someone wants to mark a special or memorable moment. You can help them leave *their* mark with *your* mark.

Writing Book Reviews
Bob Schultz

Get paid to read. Get to know your favorite authors. Get books for free. All you have to do is write book reviews. But why should a writer take time out to read and review someone *else's* novel? Why write a few hundred words of nonfiction about someone *else's* book instead of adding a few hundred words to your own project?

The answer is simple: I read books and write reviews to learn the secrets of good — and bad — writing, to stay on top of the market by reading what sells, and to make contacts with other working writers. By analyzing books and writing reviews, I'm learning what works and what doesn't in dozens of books across many genres, and that's making me a better writer. Because of the reviews I've published, I have been able to correspond with such authors as Gore Vidal, Robin Cook, Dee Brown, Greg Mcdonald and Richard Adams. I even got Christmas cards from Ray Bradbury and Louise Erdrich!

READING, THEN WRITING

First I read as a reader, but then I *reread* as a reviewer. When I take notes as I read a book for the first time, I feel like I'm preparing for a test in school. The artificiality of note taking robs much of the joy from reading. It also tends to focus my attention on trivia rather than on the whole book. Instead, read the entire book first with your eyes open for major themes, use of language, style and character development. When you come across a great quote or powerful passage that you might use in the review, make a mental note of its placement on the page so you can find it later. Remember, for example, that the description of the roller-coaster ride was in the upper-left corner of the page in about the middle of the book just before a chapter break. If I'm afraid I might not be able to find something again, I may write down a page number, but nothing more.

After the first reading, put the book down for a day or two and think about its major strengths and weaknesses. Then, with paper in hand, skim back over the book — this time taking notes. Write the page numbers in the left margin, and list any facts or quotes that might improve your review.

This method may take more time, but the results will be worth it. When I sent a review to Dee Brown, author of *Bury My Heart at Wounded Knee* (Buccaneer Books), he responded, "You may not have any idea how many reviewers skim books and then reveal how many details they missed by making some caustic comments about the failure of the author to do this or that."

Don't you make that mistake.

Your next step is to determine what made this book worth reading. Was it stylish writing, great characters, heart-stopping suspense, insightful revelations about controversial events, side-splitting humor? Begin your review by illuminating that strength. When I read Louise Erdrich's *Tracks* (HarperCollins), I was struck by the power of her prose and opened my review with *"Tracks* is a novel of sensual earthy power that crackles with crisp emotions and a potent mixture of hope and despair," to express that feeling.

In contrast, I began my review of Morris Dee's autobiography by retelling a frightening episode in the civil rights lawyer's life. My goal was to illustrate the exciting and dangerous life readers would encounter in the book. I opened with a Burns and Allen comedy routine for a chronicle of their radio shows. Just as a query letter must reflect the writing style of the piece you are proposing, a book review should match the style and strengths of the book it is reviewing.

Be cautious, however, about just how much you reveal. You've seen those movie trailers that show four hilarious scenes, and then discovered that those were the only funny scenes in the movie. Don't give away all the humor or too many clues about the final outcome. You're trying to get people to read the book, not eliminating their need to.

I also use a variation on the old fiction writer's maxim: Quote, don't tell. Let the author's words — not your descriptions — show the book's power. For example, I could say that Ray Bradbury is a prose stylist, or I could use this quote:

> The long clattering clack and grind, the ascending slow clang, rattle and roar, like some robot centipede of immense age scaling the side of a nightmare, pausing at the top for the merest breath,

then cascading in a serpentine of squeal, rush, and thunderous roar, in human shriek down the abysmal span, there to attack, more swiftly this time, another hell, another ascending scale rising yet higher and higher to fall off into hysteria.

Though this was the longest sentence I ever quoted, it showed Bradbury's style as my words could never do.

Quotes are also critical in humor reviews. When I review works by people such as columnist Lewis Grizzard, I quote extensively to show the kind of humor in the book. Grizzard's questions, such as, "When a person loses weight, where does it go?" and his idea to "sell off North Dakota, Montana, and that silly looking top part of Idaho" to pay off the national debt, would lose their edge if I tried to restate them.

Quotes also give reviewers a chance to point out weaknesses in writing and character. Because there was little I agreed with about the antics of Indiana University basketball coach Bobby Knight as I read his biography, I simply repeated some of his outrageous quotes and let readers draw their own conclusions.

The most important element of writing book reviews, however, is being able to find a theme of a book and to persuasively express it. That alone will show your strength as a reader and reviewer.

Look closely at the beginning and ending of the book. Look for recurring situations, phrases or problems that characters face. If you are familiar with the author's other works, or other works in the genre, note the similarities among the books. Find the glue that holds the book together.

I found the spirit of Camilla Carr's *Topsy Dingo Wild Dog* (Carol Publishing Group) in quotes she used from *The Velveteen Rabbit*, so I framed my review with comments about that book, beginning with a brief description of the story and ending with the comment "The Skin Horse never said becoming real was going to be easy." Carr responded by calling mine "the quintessential review"; she continued, "You didn't miss anything—no other critic even mentioned *The Velveteen Rabbit*."

Even when reviewing short story collections, I focus on themes. Daniel Stern, author of *Twice Told Tales* (W.W. Norton), said my review "singles out the process, not merely the incidents, and deals with the book's enterprise as a whole in a rich, insightful manner." Authors write with a deeper purpose than just stringing words together, and the reviewer owes it to the readers to find that deeper purpose.

CONNECTING WITH READERS

Make it clear that the book makes a connection to readers' lives in some compelling way. When John Madden wrote, "Around the house I'm a mechanical moron. I just know that if I tried to put in a light switch, I'd blow the house up," he made an immediate connection with legions of hapless do-it-yourselfers. Look for the little things that bring the book to life and make a reader feel at home within its pages.

If you find anything to connect the book to the part of the country you review from, use it. Readers shared the chill I felt when I read in a Peter Maas book that twenty tons of plastic explosives had been illegally trucked past the nearby hospital where my three children — and the children of many of my readers — were born.

You can also use the locations in the books to market your reviews in those locales. If you read a great book set in Cleveland, for instance, send a review to *The Plain Dealer* in that city. Make sure to point out the Cleveland connection.

Another way to draw readers into your reviews is to *personalize*. Sometimes you can make connections between your own life and the book. I began my review of the biography of the Wright Brothers, by Fred Howard, by writing:

> As a boy in Ohio in the 1950s there were a few facts of life that seemed eternal. Christopher Columbus discovered America, Ike would always be President, the Dodgers would never leave Brooklyn, no one would ever break Babe Ruth's records, and the Wright Brothers were the first people ever to fly.

That connected the book to anyone who remembered the 1950s and made readers wonder whether this book was going to take away one more eternal truth.

Be cautious when personalizing, however. Remember that you want to use personal experience only when your comments will enhance readers' understanding of or identification with the book you are reviewing. You aren't a columnist, you're a reviewer, so keep the focus on the book.

GETTING YOUR REVIEW RECEIVED

Before you can write reviews, you'll need to find books to review. When you're breaking into the field, you'll probably have to buy your own books, but once you're established with a publication, the editor will likely supply you with books to review. I simply stop at the editorial office whenever I have time to read a book and pick out a couple that look interesting. An advantage to getting books from a newspaper or magazine is that they receive review copies several weeks before the book is released so that the review can be written and in print when the book appears in local bookstores.

Before you send your review to an editor, study several issues of the review section of the target publication. You need to know the types of books reviewed, the average lengths of the reviews published, whether or not most reviews are staff written, and how current the books are that are reviewed. Call the publication to find out the name (and get the correct spelling) of the book review editor. It's likely that that person writes some reviews, so track those down to use as models for your own review. Your goal should be to write a review of a current book on the short side of the length range.

Another way in the door is to find a specialty you have that staff members don't share. Are you a teacher, a lawyer, a doctor or a stay-at-home mother who will understand that book about education, law, medicine or child-rearing better than the staff members can? Have you run in a marathon, gone ballooning, served on a hung jury or lived in Alaska? Review a new book that allows you to emphasize your specialty with phrases such as, "As I discovered during my twenty years of teaching . . ." or "The author captured the pain and thrill that all long-distance runners experience when she. . . ."

Stay in close contact with local colleges, bookstores and writers' clubs so you will know when authors will be speaking, signing books or conducting workshops. Then, when those authors come to town, get in to see them and note everything they say. If tapes of the speech are sold, buy one so you can get your quotes straight. Or, if it's allowed, tape it yourself. The power of being able to write, "When I asked the author about the new novel, she said . . ." or "The author said he received several death threats when the Ku Klux Klan learned about his exposé," may be just enough to entice an editor to print your review.

Though specializing is a good way to get your foot in the door, you'll need to expand your repertoire if you don't want to get stuck reviewing only that one book on orchid raising that comes out each decade. Once you've sold a few reviews, try a book totally outside your specialty genre. Show editors that you're a good reviewer, not just a good reviewer of science fiction or true crime stories.

The pay for reviews isn't much, but the intangible rewards are great. Don't spend any more time thinking that you'll write a review some day. Follow the tips I've outlined and get your review into print! You're only the price of a stamp away from starting a new phase in your writing career.

Breaking Into the Magazine Market

Maxine Rock

There's a wide range of opportunities in magazine writing simply because there are *so many* periodicals in circulation. Almost any hobby or profession — from jogging to trial law — has its own magazine.

Magazine writing is right for you if you love leafing through everything from *McCall's* to *Log House Living*, not only devouring the text, but also noticing the ads, the photos and illustrations — even the quality of the magazine's paper. If you're a magazine person, piling magazines everywhere and refusing to toss away even the most dog-eared issue, you can probably write for magazines, too — especially if you indulge in the hobby or practice the profession covered by the magazine you want to sell to.

My first major sale — to the travel section of *The New York Times* — allowed me to cash in on one of my interests. My article was about horseback riding through Yellowstone National Park, and I wrote it on muddy yellow legal paper around a campfire, with a pesty horse nibbling at my pen. Huddled by the crackling fire, I couldn't resist recording my delight over the vast, wheat-colored plains, the eagles soaring overhead, the grunts and steam floating up from the wandering bands of buffalo.

In a way, writing that article was like writing a long, colorful letter to a relative. Fine. All those heartfelt descriptions are the flesh and blood of any good magazine piece. But what editors — and readers — really want is a solid skeleton of *facts*. In this case, anybody leafing through the travel section who was captured by my description of the trip would be furious if I also didn't tell them how much it cost, how long it took, whether you had to be an experienced rider to participate, what I ate and wore, and where to write for reservations.

Do all those mundane facts take the romance out of writing? Oh, maybe just a little. Do they pay off? You bet! Almost as an afterthought, I included such information when I got home and transferred my story to neatly typed words on white bond. The *Times* editor wrote me: "I'm putting the solid stuff — costs, travel time, etc. — in the second paragraph. Without it, you've got an essay, or a rather lovely letter to a friend. We don't pay for essays or letters. But with hard facts, you've got a magazine article. So here's our check for $500."

Pardon the pun, but I learned right then that giving the facts in a magazine piece is just plain horse sense. Magazine writing can be vivid, dramatic, even heart-wrenching — but it must also be accurate, informative and thorough. Strengthen your writing with facts, and they will transform your "essays" or "letters" into money-making articles.

WHAT MAGAZINES WILL ACCEPT MY WORK?

New writers often make the mistake of trying to sell only to the big magazines, mass-circulation giants such as *Ladies Home Journal* and *Better Homes and Gardens*. But your best bet for breaking in is the smaller, specialty magazines. Go to the library and browse the periodical shelves, noting small magazines that cover subjects you know about. Do you love John Lennon's music and would you enjoy researching an article about his childhood? Then maybe you can sell to *Beatlefan*, a bimonthly from Georgia that grooves on such topics. Did you find a clever way to coax your retired husband into waxing the kitchen floor? Tell it to *Modern Maturity*, whose editors will pay you for such information. You can find some of these specialty magazines on the newsstands in major cities or in large bookstores. Others are available only to subscribers or people who ask for a copy. Bookstores also carry *Writer's Market*, a directory published by Writer's Digest Books, containing names, addresses and descriptions of almost every magazine in North America. The directory is a worthwhile investment, but it's best to have the magazine you want to sell to in hand if you want to learn enough about it to make a sale. (*Writer's Market* will tell you if the magazine sends sample issues to potential contributors.) Once you have selected your target magazines, read at least three back copies of each in the library. Then buy the most recent issues and get acquainted with your future markets.

When you read those magazines, you'll be doing market research. First, read each story until you have a firm grasp of the tone and presentation used by the magazines' writers. Are they big on humor?

Do the articles start with little anecdotes, or is the information presented in a straightforward, no-nonsense format? Count the number of words in the articles. Is equal space given to every topic, or does the magazine have one or two long features and five or six small fillers?

Check the *masthead*, which is the listing of editors' names usually found in the front of the magazine. If the names on the masthead are the same as the bylines on the articles, this magazine may be staff-written and won't accept freelance material. If the bylines belong to people whose names are not listed up front, you can make a sale.

Don't overlook the ads. By reading them, you can tell a lot about the type of people who read the magazine and what subjects the editors need to keep these readers informed and entertained. Do the ads show smartly dressed men and women climbing into sleek sports cars? Then this is a magazine for upscale folks who'd probably like articles on fine wines, expensive furniture or good private schools. If the ads show young families, or housewives squeezing the Charmin, its readers probably care about the effects of TV violence on youngsters and ways to save money at the supermarket. All these topics can be geared to the magazine's specialty. If you're looking at *Bicycling* magazine, for example, you might think about a piece on nutrition for cyclists, emphasizing the new health-food sections now springing up in chain supermarkets.

Ideas like these will come to you as you study the magazine. I feel strongly that the best way to make money at article writing is not to have an idea and then find a magazine to suit it, but to find a suitable magazine and *then* let the ideas flow. Why? Because it's easier that way. You can have an idea on how to lure songbirds to your garden by planting the vegetation they favor, but unless you know the magazine market, it can take weeks to track down *Blair and Ketchum's Country Journal*, which might publish your article on the topic. It is certainly possible to have an idea and find a potentially suitable magazine market by looking at the subject listings in *Writer's Market*. But editors and magazines constantly change, and you must be familiar with recent issues to develop a gut feeling about the subject matter they prefer, as well as the style and audience. It is also crucial to not propose an idea the magazine has recently covered. I learned that the hard way, from the editor of *National Geographic*. We were chatting over dinner at a writers' conference, and when he invited me to submit article ideas, I fished an outline on gorillas out of my purse and presented it to him proudly.

The editor dabbed at the corners of his mouth with his napkin and said, "If you'd *read* us lately, you'd see we had a piece on gorillas two issues ago."

Gulp. The lamb chop I had just eaten twirled madly in my stomach. I had violated one of my own primary rules: Read back issues of the magazine before you try to sell to it. I won't do that again. My digestion can't take it.

HOW DO I GET MY IDEAS ACROSS TO EDITORS?

I don't usually present outlines to editors over dinner (or lunch). And I know that editors hate phone calls because most of them like to read more than they like to talk. So, if you have an idea for an article, write a query letter. A query is a question, and the question you're asking the editor is, "Would you like to buy a magazine article based on this idea?" The query letter should start with a strong first paragraph that is as close as possible to the way you'd start the article itself. In paragraph two, explain how you'd develop the idea and give your sources of information. Next, devote a paragraph to telling the editor why you're qualified to do the job: You're a lifelong bird-watcher, for example, who has drawn thirty-two different varieties of songbirds to the neighborhood through proper planting. You don't have to have prior bylines, but if you have had anything published, it helps to send along a photocopy of your work. Make sure the letter is neatly typed on good white bond paper, and include a self-addressed, stamped envelope (SASE) to speed the editor's reply.

That reply might come in one of several forms. Some editors like to phone a potential contributor, either to say, "We love your idea and we'll buy it," or to ask for more information before they make a decision. A phone call from an editor is a good sign of genuine interest. Most often, however, a letter will be used as a contract to spell out exactly what is wanted (length, deadline, method of approach) and what you'll get in return (when and how much you'll be paid, and some guarantee of partial payment if the idea doesn't work, which is called a *kill fee*). Be prepared, also, for a form rejection letter or a personal note telling you that while the idea is good, the editors just don't feel it is right for them at this moment. Anytime you get personal encouragement of this sort, consider yourself to have been noticed as a potential writer for the magazine and hit them with another idea fast — before they forget your name.

New writers often ask me what they should do with manuscripts they have already prepared, before they realized that magazine editors like to hear ideas first, make assignments and then receive the finished product. If you just couldn't resist writing a story and want to sell it and see it in print, run for your *Writer's Market*. Magazines are listed there by category, such as religious, medical, home and garden, or regional. You may find several good candidates for your article. Write to them one by one, explain the topic, and tell the editor that while you have a full manuscript already prepared, you'd be willing to revise it if necessary to fit the magazine's format. Don't send the full manuscript. That's expensive and often overwhelms the editor.

Payment for articles varies widely, from $5 for a book review to $3,500 for a human-interest drama. New writers can expect an average of $125-$300 for their efforts; experienced professionals command thousands per article from major magazines. Small magazines usually pay less, but remember that your chances of success there are far greater than if you tried to compete with big names selling to the major market. Little by little — if you're persistent and your talent shines through — you can ask for and receive fee increases from magazine editors who get to know your work.

Magazine writing differs from that done for books not only because payment is far less for a much shorter product. You must also choose a very specific topic for a magazine, make your point quickly, back it up with research and quotes from experts, and conclude. Most magazine editors will give you a word limit — and take it from me, they're *serious* about it. If they ask for 2,500 words, that's almost exactly what they want. Give them more, and they'll cut your article. Give them less, and you'll hear them howl, "Where's the rest?" With books you can go longer, explore many facets of your subject and analyze several potential conclusions. Magazines simply don't have the space to indulge you in this way.

Some editors ask for an article outline before they'll actually assign you to do the writing. Don't be afraid to fire back a concise, well-planned outline, double-spaced on one or two pages. Tell *exactly* how you will approach the article. In my outlines, I usually include a dramatic lead or opening paragraph. Under it, I write a sentence to describe each point I will make to bolster my opening statement. Then, another brief paragraph contains the main point of the body of the piece, and several numbered sentences support this premise and show the research I intend to do. A third paragraph is my summary.

Presenting an outline shows that you've already put a lot of thought—and some research—into the endeavor, and reassures the editor that you really do know what you're talking about. If you're a new writer, or simply new to that editor, his request for an outline is reasonable. After all, if he assigns a piece and you can't deliver, he's spent a lot of time and trouble and may have to quickly find a replacement. Worse, he may print your piece only to be deluged with angry letters from readers who dispute your information and cancel subscriptions. An outline is simply an editor's way of saying: "Give me more information on this. Show me I can trust you."

TRUST?

Speaking of trust, it works both ways. The editor will tell you how many words to write, when she wants you to hand in the story (your deadline), and when you'll be paid and how much; she may even coach you on how to organize your material and on ways to present it in the most appealing way possible. She trusts you to obey all these instructions and to take her advice to heart. And every editor expects a neatly typed manuscript on clean white $8\frac{1}{2}'' \times 11''$ bond paper, accompanied by a covering letter that recaps the story and reminds the editor of previous correspondence. Editors deal with up to twenty writers a day. Often, they can't immediately remember the articles they have assigned, or who is writing them.

You must nevertheless trust the editor to read your finished piece carefully, change or delete material only when absolutely necessary, consult you about such changes, and let you see a galley proof before publication. This means that you'll be sent the edited version of your article, on rough paper, so you can see exactly what it will look like in print. This way you have a chance to put in your two cents if you don't approve of something the editor has done. If you have a reasonable gripe, a good editor will certainly pay attention.

That's the ideal editorial process. But there are plenty of horror stories about writers who sent in a good manuscript only to have an editor revise it so drastically (without telling them) that they didn't recognize their own work when it was printed. I always ask for author's galleys, but sometimes I don't get them. Once an editor not only misspelled the name of a doctor I had interviewed, but also got his specialty wrong and took his quotes entirely out of context! Naturally, the doctor was furious with *me* when the story appeared, and I had some fancy explaining to do. I complained to the editor, but she just mumbled, "Sorry 'bout that."

There's really no way to protect yourself from such embarrassing situations except to deal with reputable people and do your best to secure an author's galley. Experience will teach you which editors are good and which to avoid.

Experience will also give you a realistic concept of how much you can earn yearly from freelance nonfiction magazine article writing. I have been a professional in this field full time for eight years, and before that I wrote part time for twelve years and supplemented my income by teaching journalism at a university. When I was a part-timer, the most I ever made from my writing was $14,000 per year; the least was $3,000. Full time, my lowest annual income has been $13,000 and my highest $45,000. To get information on yearly incomes for this article, I polled several of my writing peers in Atlanta and New York City. We all publish at least two major articles per month, plus a column or brief story, restaurant review or book review. We all have advanced journalism degrees and at least fifteen years of experience. The average income is about $35,000 yearly, made by working at least eight and sometimes twelve or fifteen hours each weekday.

You may never want to work that hard at writing — and you don't have to. The wonderful thing about magazine writing is being your own boss, setting your own hours and having the freedom to explore topics that fascinate you. You can write a little bit and make a little bit of money — or you can go at it full time and hope to hit the top.

Traveling the Lucrative Road of Travel Writing

Christopher P. Baker

If you're a travel writer, or want to be one, sharing sojourns is your business. Placing readers on some mountaintop or beach is a prescription for making money from that Mexican vacation, African safari or Greek island cruise you took last summer.

A successful travel article does more than conjure up unforgettable images and lead readers by the hand. It entertains, provides reliable and useful information, and tells the truth. But if you fail to place your reader vicariously on that mountaintop or on that beach you've described, you will not sell your article in this highly competitive market.

Providing readers with a shared feeling for a destination is the essence of good travel writing. Even roundup pieces (such as "The Ten Best Romantic Hideaways") and other purely informational features need spicing with the presence and ambience of a place. Tepid travelogues offering blow-by-blow accounts won't do. Appeal to your readers' senses and incite an emotional response. In doing so, you breathe *possibility* into your readers' own travel plans — and make your destinations come alive.

James Boswell, the eighteenth-century Scottish biographer, wrote that "the use of traveling is to regulate imagination by reality, and instead of thinking how things may be, to see them as they really are." Here are four techniques I use to take readers by the hand and show them how the places I visit really are.

CREATE AN IMMEDIATE IMAGE

As in any writing genre, your beginning should arouse as well as interest. It should excite readers and compel them to read on. But as a travel writer, you must also create an enduring vision of your destination if you're to grab your readers' interests.

Consider this opening:

> "There," someone screamed, tapping the window so hard I thought it would break. "Everest!"
>
> To our left, as we looked above the gray haze of the valley below, the Himalayas stretched away as far as the eye could see: a ragged escarpment of arrowheads tipped with a sprinkling of white.
>
> A blackened face rose above them, peering through the fading rose-tinged mist of early morn. Everest. That uninspired yet unmistakable pyramid of rock, with its veil of courtesan cloud trailing behind, guarded by the spires of Nuptse and Lhotse gleaming like shiny-armored sentinels in a dazzling royal blue sky.

In this article—a personal-experience piece about hiking in the Himalayas—I open at the moment that matters most: when the highest peak on earth first comes into view. There's drama in the opening sentence. The emotion is obvious. The reader is already there, drawn by the excitement of anticipation aboard the aircraft, and by a shared suspense broken when the clouds finally part, and a lifelong dream is fulfilled. He can envision being among the celestial heights. (Newspaper editors thought so, too. The 1,200-word piece sold fifteen times.)

For a personal-experience piece—where you relive your own adventure or trip in anecdotal account—you can easily arouse readers' interests by getting the action going straight away. Seduce readers with the climactic moment, when the suspense is at a peak.

In my Everest story, the climactic moment coincidentally happens to be at the beginning of the trip. It could as easily have been when Everest next came into view, on the third day on the trail—or when awakening on the last day of the trek "to be blessed by a cloudless sunrise, for I had climbed a treacherous trail by the light of the gossamer moon to gain a vantage for the dawn." The important thing is to use whatever moment pulls your reader *immediately* into the picture.

Not all narrative will begin at a moment of drama, of course, especially if you're writing about a week spent dozing on the beach or if you're describing the attractions of a resort on some remote Pacific isle. If you're writing a mood piece that lacks action, you still must create an immediate image.

In the opening to a feature on Katmandu for *Far East Traveler*, for example, I chose a strong image and a specific moment as pegs to make the reader feel immediately involved in the scene:

> Dawn in Katmandu. A lone figure kneels beside a shrine, his velvety form a silhouette from a mystic dreamworld in the primeval hiatus where moonlit shadows are dissolved in a veil of golden light, as though this were the very dawn of Creation itself. It is a transcendental moment.
>
> As the pencils of dawn's rays stream through the alleyways, devotees emerge carrying ritual offerings — puja — to wake up their multiple gods at sacred temples with soft-whispered prayers that carry upon the silence of first light.

In this example, I give life to the world I'm describing and create a powerful image for my reader to use as a reference point to read on. Katmandu comes alive. Provide an image for your reader to see, touch and smell his surroundings. In other words, set the scene for the reader's involvement.

Travel, after all, is about *place*. Even the most exciting travel experience will fall flat when put to paper if it happens in a vacuum. You must identify the personality of the destination — in Katmandu's case, an ancient spirituality — and create a picture that depicts the essence of that destination by combining applied imagination with personal experience. In short, get to the heart of your destination's character. Close your eyes and take yourself back. What is the single most interesting element of the place or experience? What moment stands out? Relive that moment and the emotion you felt. Then put it to words. It will give your destination character and a reference point — an image — from which to proceed. And your readers will be by your side.

MAP OUT THE JOURNEY

After you've hooked your readers, let them know why they should read on. As with all articles, travel articles need a slant, an identity, to set limits in which to present your subject. Otherwise, your subject could spill in all directions, like liquid without a container. Even the travel article that promises "everything you need to know about . . ." needs a focus to hold it together. Let your reader know, up front, what that special angle is.

In my Katmandu piece — having provided a strong image as a hook — I tell the readers that I'm going to lead them by the hand on a walking tour of the city's historic heart:

Visitors to this ancient capital of the tiny Himalayan kingdom of Nepal will find themselves stepping back in time, crossing the threshold to another dimension. Gone are the hippies of the psychedelic 1960s who came, in the wake of the Beatles, seeking hashish and Hindu and Buddhist enlightenment. But the sublime attractions remain.

As in medieval times, the hub of the city is Durbar Square, whose fifty or so temples and shrines imbue it with an aura of religious mystique.

A perfect starting point for a walking tour of the city's heart is the Kasthamandap, the "House of Wood," on Durbar's southwest corner. Erected in the twelfth century. . . .

My readers soon know that they're going to be informed, as well as entertained. Informing your reader is a *sine qua non* for selling travel articles. Editors demand it. You needn't tell your reader about every king and queen who slept in a hotel's four-poster bed, or the best place to buy a souvenir for Aunt Maude. But you do need to furnish the piece with enough factual information to add authority and legitimacy. And don't be afraid to be honest about what you've found.

As you write, don't forget service information. In the past few years, magazines like *Travel & Leisure* and *Condé Nast Traveler* have moved from the sophisticated and general to the specific, not only guiding readers through the backstreets of London, but also telling them what shoes to wear and where to pop in for the best cream tea in town. Most markets now want a healthy dose of service information to flesh out and add a dimension of usefulness to even the most entertaining destination piece.

Mapping out an article's identity also helps you balance the narrative and the service information, and keeps the article from degenerating into a prosaic where-to and how-to account — unless that's what the editor wants. (If you fear including too much service information, put the how-to-get-there, where-to-eat nitty-gritty in a sidebar. Many editors prefer that style of presentation.)

Travel writing shares much with other genres. Fiction writers, for example, can teach the travel writer about moving facts and events around to create "breathless expectation of development," in the words of travel writer Louise Purwin Zobel. Craft the chronology of your article to suit your plot and to add vitality and impact to your story. A travelogue written in rigid chronological fashion is about as exhilarating as taking a roller-coaster ride without the dips and falls.

Likewise, even those articles written for the reader who demands to be saturated with historical tidbits, the lowdown on where to eat, and exact directions will bore if you don't add life and vitality to a piece. Remember the professor in *Never on Sunday* who went to Greece to look at the ruins but discovered the real Greece while dancing in a tavern.

SHOW, DON'T TELL

The ability to share travel experiences with others relies on your skill in painting strong and sensual pictures with words. As travel writer Robert Scott Milne says: "Everything a travel writer feels about a place or its people must be seized on and fully realized in words." How did the bougainvilleas *smell*?" What were the *sounds* of Naples at night? How did it *feel* to savor the silence of the Sahara? Were the mountains just "there," or did they "pierce the sky"? Did the waterfalls merely "fall," or did they "cascade in ribbons of quicksilver"? And was the forest "thick" or "vibrant and insatiable"? Reproducing the experience or mood in flavorful, sensual detail will give spontaneity and life to your writing. According to Apa Productions' *Insight Guide*, Jamaica, for example:

> . . . is hard to resist. There's something sensuous in its curvaceous contour, in the way the winds tease the palms and the waves lick upon the shore. There's a beguiling quality to its reggae rhythms and its people's lilting patois. Jamaica has had this persuasive effect for centuries. Once it seduces you, it might not let go. . . .

Simile and metaphor are essential tools for the travel writer. In Nepal, for example, I "peek at the Milky Way cast across the void of sky like a handful of silvery stardust on a canvas of India ink." Varanasi, in India, ". . . seems to ache with age and penury, like a palimpsest, written upon and imperfectly erased again and again." And at dawn, Bryce Canyon in Utah is ". . . bathed in the warmth of the sun, and the majestic forms, immersed in deepening sanguine light, come to life like a Polaroid shot developing before one's eyes."

Ache. Bathed. Immersed. Such active verbs give energy and movement to your prose, like bright pastels added to an artist's dull canvas. No one wants to be told what somewhere is like. They want to be shown. Armchair travelers have only their imaginations as guides.

Stimulate them by describing the sights and smells and sounds vividly and in intricate, perceptive detail to create an enduring vision — one that leaves readers with a sense of having discovered that destination for themselves. Choosing words that carry their own destinational flavor and cultural allusion helps, too. An injection of Greek words — *meltemi, souflaki* — will aid in transporting your readers to the fabled birthplace of the *Iliad* and the *Odyssey*, for example.

Be careful, though, of injecting a false epic quality in an attempt to turn journalism into literature. Travel writing lends itself to the traps of excessive praise, using unnecessary adjectives and even misrepresentation. Use graphic language to develop word pictures, but leave hackneyed words like *spectacular* and *gorgeous* to the brochure copywriters. As Hemingway said, "eschew the monumental." It's the small details that count, so record them with a meticulous eye. And record the emotions, too. I write my notes in sentence form to capture the mood of a moment completely. Later, it's easy to pick out the scattered beads, string them together and polish them till they shine.

PROVIDE A TRAVELING COMPANION

Narrative without a human element is like pasta without spice: all texture and no taste. Anecdote and dialogue add seasoning and zest. They enliven the pace, engage the eye and provide drama and character, so that readers feel the warmth of the human touch and are drawn by the personal contact and the sense of a story shared. Dialogue also works well as a tool for adding personality and humor, while a well-chosen anecdote or two can dramatize your angle and reinforce your theme.

Consider my opening for a feature on bicycle touring in Utah for *Westways* magazine:

> Most written descriptions cannot hint at the bewitching effect Bryce Canyon National Park has on the first-time visitor. Its elaborate spires and colonnades seem less the random work of Nature than the surrealistic sculptures of some primeval Michelangelo, its brilliant colors the impressionistic whimsy of some animated God.
>
> For cyclists puffing hard up the nine-mile climb through Red Canyon, the salmon walls dancing in the heat of Utah's late summer give a foretaste of the delight to come.

"A geologist's dream," chimed one 69-year-old on a seven-day cycling tour of America's southwest.

Cresting a final, short rise, she let out an almighty sigh. "It's enchanting!" she exclaimed. "I wouldn't have done this any other way." Appropriately she had stopped above Fairyland Trail.

Adding the personal touch allowed my readers to share the emotional impact from a second source. It added authority and strength to my claim, plus a lightness to keep the narrative dancing.

If you're not in the story yourself, include somebody else — even your reader. Using the second person puts your reader *immediately* in the story. In *Preferred Traveler*, I used it as a guide to lead my readers around the Greek island of Ios: "With luck, the paths may lead you to a quiet cove backed by fig trees, where the water is warm. Here, you should rest beneath the shade of an old fig tree, contemplating your muse, until the sizzle of the cicadas and the pleasing odors of lemons and vines drive you to sleep."

But use second person sparingly. Overused, it becomes a substitute for the hard work of otherwise making your destination come alive. Properly used — in conjunction with the other tools and tips I've presented here — it helps you share with the reader the intimate appeal of destinations both exotic and mundane. It allows you to take your reader along with you.

Cashing In on Your Hobbies

Michael A. Banks

Sometimes I'm not sure what my neighbors think I do for a living. I'm a full-time writer, but, more often than not, when someone drops by, I can be found reading a new science fiction novel, playing a computer game or launching model rockets. Playing, you see, is a part of my work — because I get paid to write about my hobbies.

I've always been involved in at least one hobby, and I've always sought out books and articles about my leisure-time pursuits. In many instances, I found that the hobby books in print fell short (they didn't tell me anything new), and that books I would have liked to read didn't exist. So, after my early writing began to see print, I started producing the books and articles I couldn't find. I've enjoyed reasonable success at this, and the research is lots of fun. I've written a dozen articles, a magazine column and three books on model rocketry — "the eighty-seventh most popular hobby in the United States." I've also written about more mundane topics, such as collecting stamps and first-day covers.

My hobbies may not seem as esoteric as yours, but remember there are also books on such "esoteric" topics as building mobiles, kite-building and designing your own airplane. There are titles in print on narrow topics like photographing scale models and building dioramas. And I have friends who write about such arcane topics as pinball machines and collecting pulp magazines.

Of course, most hobby articles and books are about more familiar hobbies such as model railroading, stained glass window art and coin collecting. But, arcane or mundane, these articles and books have one thing in common — they are almost always written by active hobbyists.

Where can you write about your hobby? There are three basic markets: magazines, book publishers and hobby manufacturers.

MAGAZINES

General-interest magazines — ranging from Sunday supplements to men's magazines — sometimes carry overview or introductory articles about hobbies. You're more likely to sell this kind of article if you're involved in something really fascinating or timely, like astronomy or antique auto racing, but a good writer can make almost any hobby interesting.

When writing about your hobby for a general-interest magazine, remember that readers don't want to be told everything about your hobby. A general-interest article should merely highlight the more interesting aspects of the hobby, and perhaps cover the basics of getting into it. For example, when I wrote articles about model rocketry for *Daybreak* and *Science Digest*, my goal was to pass along some interesting information (about aerial photography and international competition) and maybe gain a convert or two along the way.

On the other hand, writing for specialized magazines that are published solely for people engaged in a particular hobby gives you the opportunity to go into much more detail about your hobby. And there is a larger market in writing for these publications. Check the Hobby and Craft section of *Writer's Market* to find out about magazines that deal with the hobby you're involved in.

To write about your hobby for other hobbyists, you really have to know your stuff. A small percentage of your audience will know as much or more about your hobby than you do — and they are usually the people who like to write letters catching writers' mistakes. Editors of hobby publications know their readers are looking for solid information and new ideas, and that's what they expect from their writers.

Here's a quick rundown of the kinds of articles hobby magazines are looking for:

You will find a limited market among specialized magazines for *introductory* or *overview articles*. Most of these magazines are operated on the assumption that the average reader is already involved in the hobby, and thus knows the jargon and other basics. Still, they may run articles aimed at beginners from time to time, to cater to new readers.

The mainstay of magazines that deal with "hands-on" hobbies is the *project article*; many readers buy magazines just for the projects they contain. Using step-by-step instructions, and sometimes drawings and plans, this kind of article shows the reader how to complete a particular project — a model airplane, a quilt, etc.

Another staple is the *technique instruction article*, which helps the reader learn or improve a skill that can be applied to more than one project. Salvaging and mounting stamps for display, cleaning coins and preserving old books are topics typical of those covered in technique instruction articles.

New product articles, *book articles* and *reviews* offer another outlet. Writing them is probably the easiest way to break into the hobby market. (An added bonus: You generally get to keep the product or book after writing the piece.)

If you belong to a group or club devoted to your hobby, you may find a market for *group activity reports*. Model aircraft magazines regularly carry reports of local and regional competitions and shows, and collectors' magazines feature information on swap meets and auctions. (One of my collaborators, who writes on antiques and collectibles, picks up a fair spare-time income by covering antique shows and auctions in the South for *Carolina Antique News* — expenses paid.)

Less frequently used, but usually sought after, are *hobbyist profiles*, especially of well-known, successful competitors and craftspersons. Articles about old-timers have appeal, too; if you happen to know someone who has been involved in your hobby for many years, you may well find him or her a fascinating source of historical information, as well as of human interest material.

Some hobby magazines also run *research pieces* consisting of straight factual or historical background — say, on how bank note engravings are made, aimed at collectors of paper money. Pieces dealing with the history of the hobby, or with related history (such as the growth of passenger rail service in the West, for model railroad hobbyists), also fit into this category.

Marketing your hobby articles to magazines should be done just as you would market any other article — via a query letter. You will find, however, that the editors of hobby-specific magazines are easier to deal with than other editors. They are almost always hobbyists themselves and are often open to informal telephone queries.

Pay rates among hobby magazines are about $.05 to $.08 per word. Most of these magazines pay by the article or printed page, though, with separate payment for photos.

BOOKS

Like the magazine market, the market for hobby books breaks down into two types — introductory and specialized. Introductory books are most commonly published by large trade book publishers. On the other hand, specialized, or advanced, books are aimed at people who read the hobby-specific magazines and are usually published by specialty publishers such as Kalmbach Books, TAB Books and Arco, which have the kind of distribution systems — via hobby shops, mail order and other means, in addition to normal bookstores — that can reach those dedicated hobbyists.

The market size for an introductory hobby book depends on how many other introductory books there are on the subject and the hobby's popularity. There is a lot of room for beginner's books on model railroading and stamp collecting, for instance, because so many people are involved in these hobbies. On the other hand, the market for introductory books on knife collecting is limited — both because several books in print already meet the needs of this market and because not as many people collect knives.

The amount of change a hobby undergoes affects how salable a beginner's book is likely to be, too. Some hobbies, like stonecarving, don't change much over the years, while others, like model aviation, are affected by advances in technology and the changing status of manufacturers and suppliers. Thus, there's room in the market for introductory books offering up-to-date information on these subjects.

Keep the potential for change in mind when writing any sort of hobby book, because the average book appears in the stores twelve to twenty-four months after the author completes it. When discussing tips and techniques, include the latest information on what is being done by other hobbyists. When putting together book appendices that list manufacturers and other sources, list only those companies you believe are stable and will be in business for a few more years. (Often, you will be given the chance to update such listings before publication, when the book is in galley stage, but don't count on it.)

To write a specialized hobby book, you must not only show proficiency in your hobby, but also come up with new ideas. Still, there is a limit to just how specialized you can get. I could not, for example, sell a book solely about aerial photography with model rockets — there isn't enough interest in that aspect of the hobby, and there certainly isn't enough material to make a book. But that topic is a *part* of my book *Second Stage: Advanced Model Rocketry* (Kalmbach Press), which also covers other advanced hobby activities.

Advances and royalties for hobby books among trade publishers are comparable to those for other nonfiction books — $4,000 and up for advances, with royalties of about 10 percent. Specialty book publishers usually pay smaller advances — $1,000 to $2,000 — but keep their books in print longer and reach markets the big-time publishers miss.

MANUFACTURERS

Companies that manufacture hobby products are another market for writing about your hobby. Some of these companies bring out catalogs, pamphlets, manuals, magazines and other publications for their customers. I've written articles for consumer publications and catalogs that were published by model rocket manufacturers, manuals for computer games and research reports.

Catalogs are generally done in-house, but many manufacturers like to include informational or image-building articles in their publications, and these are frequently written by freelancers. Magazines that are provided free (such as Estes Industries' *Model Rocket News*) or by subscription by manufacturers are always in need of original articles. Manufacturers also need manuals to accompany their products and may publish pamphlets that are essentially introductory articles about the hobby they cater to. (Such pamphlets are especially popular among manufacturers involved in hobbies that are little-known or that involve some element of danger.) Pay rates vary widely — I've received as little as $20 for a short article to as much as $750 for a short manual.

Tapping into this market requires research and persistence, and sometimes salesmanship. To find out about companies that publish material on your hobby, acquaint yourself with the many publications available from toy and hobby manufacturers in a well-stocked hobby shop or wherever you buy your supplies. Observe what kinds of material they're publishing, come up with projects that might be appropriate for them, and approach them with your ideas. (In some cases, writers who have established themselves as knowledgeable about a particular hobby are approached by the manufacturers.)

If a hobby manufacturer already publishes a magazine for its customers, you will probably find that its editor welcomes articles from readers like yourself, but check to make sure the publication uses freelance material. A well-written query, presenting your ideas and expertise, is usually more effective in helping you land an assignment than sending a complete manuscript.

If you have an idea for a pamphlet, you are going to have to do some selling; the fact that the pamphlet doesn't exist already indicates that the manufacturer hasn't perceived a need for it. This doesn't mean you'll be turned down, but you will have to convince your potential client of the value of your idea. The best approach is to provide a proposal outlining the pamphlet and explaining who will read it and why, and how it will benefit the manufacturer to publish it. Include clips of your published work and a sample section of the proposed project.

If you wish to write instruction manuals or other material regularly published by a manufacturer, send a list of your credits and samples of your work, along with a cover letter stating your availability for such work and your experience in the hobby.

Some manufacturers also publish their own books (usually magazine-sized) dealing with *very* specialized aspects of a hobby. Specialized hobby books that might not find a market among book publishers might sell to a hobby manufacturer. For example, a book on decals is too narrow to appeal to a book publisher — even a hobby-book publisher would rather see broader coverage — but a manufacturer of decals might well want to publish such a book for its customers.

THE RIGHT CONNECTIONS AND FRINGE BENEFITS

Making contacts with manufacturers, suppliers and publishers who serve your hobby is vital if you intend to write more than one article on the hobby, and certainly if you are doing a book.

In addition to being an excellent source of research material, manufacturers can provide you with photos and camera-ready artwork to accompany your writing. (You will probably be expected to supply photos or illustrations with technique instruction or project articles, and books should be heavily illustrated — about 40 percent art to 60 percent text. Check with the market in question about specific requirements.)

Make it a point to supply your sources with copies of any magazine pieces or books you publish that mention or display their products. And don't demand too much of a source.

Keep up with everything happening in your hobby. Join local or national organizations of hobbyists in your field, and stay in touch with your manufacturer contacts. If there are trade journals for the companies that cater to your hobby, read them frequently. You may also find organizations of specific types of manufacturers. For example, most of the companies that manufacture model railroad equipment, model airplanes and the like belong to the Hobby Industry Association of America (319 E. 54th St., Elmwood Park, New Jersey 07407). Other sources of such information include the National Association of Manufacturers (1331 Pennsylvania Ave. NW, Ste. 1500 N, Washington, DC 20004) and the Toy Manufacturers of America (200 5th Ave., New York, New York 10010).

Writer's Market lists trade journals for manufacturers and retailers of a wide variety of hobby-oriented products, and your local library should have an encyclopedia of trade associations.

You may wonder if writing about your hobby takes away from the fun of it. Although I will admit I've been too busy writing about model rocketry over the past year to do much building, I've found that writing about my hobbies has enriched my activities with knowledge I might not have gained otherwise. . . . And I have more money to invest in my hobbies, too, since I've cashed in on them with my typewriter.

Where the Money Is in Business Writing

Paul M. Thompson

This is the story of Mary the magazine writer and Bill the business writer. They were both excited to get their latest assignments. Both were talented writers, and both spent considerable time researching, outlining, writing a first draft, rewriting and polishing. They were pleased with their finished products and were especially happy to be paid. Mary opened an envelope from the magazine and pulled out a check for $250. "Not bad for one assignment," she thought. Bill pulled out his $4,000 check from the ad agency. "Not bad," he said, "especially when I'm already working on a slide show to go with the marketing manual I just wrote."

Farfetched? Not at all. For the past decade, I've made my living writing business communications. I've also followed the popular writing markets, and it has never ceased to amaze me how many talented writers end up earning less than the minimum wage writing for magazines, even national ones. The same effort put into business writing would earn them five or ten times the money.

I currently work at a communications agency that regularly pays writers several thousands of dollars per assignment. Recently, we hired a writer to prepare the copy for a marketing manual introducing car dealers to a new model. We paid him $12,000. Even smaller assignments that take only a few days often net $2,000 to $3,000.

True, we're not hiring neophytes. These writers are specialists who know the auto industry and have years of experience writing for it. Still, even less experienced writers can make good money writing for business. A simple, short assignment can easily bring a new writer $1,000 or more.

WHAT IS BUSINESS WRITING?

What are these writing assignments? You see their results every day. Advertisements (print and broadcast), brochures, training manuals, speeches, research reports, newsletters, "ghost" articles — the list goes on and on. The next time you're in someone's office, look at the forms of written material on the desk and shelves. It may not be glamorous, but it *is* writing, and someone got paid to produce it.

So, is this writer's nirvana reserved for a few Madison Avenue hotshot copywriters? Not at all. It simply takes ability, persistence, patience and a willingness to market yourself to creative directors.

In larger markets, most business writing is done through agencies — advertising, public relations and the increasing number of marketing services companies that handle a variety of corporate assignments. Most agencies have two distinct divisions — the account side and the creative side. The account people work closest with the clients because they sell the agency's services. The creative side does the actual writing, and that's where your efforts will pay off.

In most cases, the assignments are supervised by a creative director, who is responsible for the final product — editorial and art. Smaller agencies may not have staff copywriters and will contract with freelancers to handle virtually all their writing work. Even those large agencies with many staff writers find that work often piles up, forcing creative directors to go outside for particularly pressing assignments.

WHO BUYS IT?

The creative director is like a magazine's editor. He or she has more work than time available, a variety of responsibilities, inflexible deadlines and a frustration at not having a big enough stable of freelancers to count on at crunch time.

A beginner gets a foot in the door with a query letter and/or phone call, followed with clips of previous work. The next steps are a personal interview and then a first assignment. If that goes well, it can mean a second call and then an ongoing relationship. At a busy agency with many clients and a constant need for new material, that relationship can prove lucrative.

Before you sit down to write, understand that business writing is much more specialized than the writing you may be used to. Just as you can't expect to write for *Modern Tire Dealer* without a knowledge of the tire industry, you can't expect to write for Goodyear or Firestone (or any other company) without a background in their business. Knowing how to write isn't enough—you must know something about the business. Therefore, start where you have some experience. If your day job is selling retail clothing, look for opportunities that allow you to make use of your experience.

HOW BUSINESS AND POPULAR WRITING DIFFER

A good writer is a good writer; if you can write a good magazine article, you can write for business. There *are* differences, however.

Business writing is more purposeful. The bottom line in business writing is much more obvious. Somewhere along the line, you are selling a product or service. *Never forget this.* It's easy to remember if you're writing a sales brochure, but even if you're writing a speech or a training manual for salespeople, the ultimate purpose for your writing is to increase sales. (*That's* why you're pulling in those big fees!)

Business writing must be more direct. Because your purpose is more clearly defined, your writing must be clear, too. Business writing puts a premium on strong, direct language. That's not to say it stifles creativity. On the contrary, creativity that sparks reader (or audience) interest will increase the number and frequency of your follow-up assignments. It's just that the flowery phrases that may impress your writing professor or your literary editor won't cut it with the client. Write forcefully, and choose your words with care.

Deadlines for business writing assignments are tighter. If you can't write under incredibly tight deadlines, forget about business writing. The new, ultraslim atomic widget is going on the market January 1, no matter what. That will mean tough deadlines, and you'll have to produce. Also, agencies often don't resort to freelancers until they realize they don't have the staff to handle a project. That usually doesn't happen until very late in the game. It's not unusual to get a phone call at 4 P.M. for an assignment that's due the next day. (But think of what that does to your hourly rate!) I know of no better way to establish a strong relationship with a creative director than to produce solid copy at a few hours' notice. Your name will be permanently etched in the director's mental Rolodex file.

Business assignments involve more politics and hassles. As a nonstaff freelancer writing for a magazine, you're fairly immune to the politics of organizations. You may have to deal with a cranky editor now and then, but usually it's one-on-one between you and the editor, and you should be able to handle most problems with patience and good telephone etiquette.

In writing for business, you'll come in contact with agency people and clients who can make your life miserable (usually because they can't write as well as you can, but refuse to admit it). Your copy may be perfect, but it will be changed because of noneditorial considerations. For instance, you write the brochure, everyone agrees that it's right on target, and then a new client complains that her part of the project didn't get enough play. She forces a rewrite, not because the original copy wasn't good, but because she has more political power in the organization. Stupid? Of course. But that kind of thing happens every day in business writing.

Business writing leaves less room for the writer's ego. If you're the kind of writer who cringes at every change an editor makes, forget the business world. Not only will the agency people change your copy several times, but when the clients get hold of it, you'll be lucky to recognize the original draft. As a business writer, you need a thick skin — and the patience to deal with people who often don't recognize good prose.

Business assignments require interpersonal skills. In writing for a magazine, you may never personally meet your editor. Not so in business. Clients usually want to meet the living, breathing person who is writing their copy, and a good relationship with the client will solidify your importance to the agency's account. Often, a less talented writer with excellent people skills will do better than a creative dynamo who doesn't have the patience to massage egos and work with difficult clients.

Production values are more important in business writing. In writing for popular media, you usually aren't concerned with the final layout because that's handled by art directors, whom you never see, at the magazine. In business writing, however, it's to your advantage to understand the production requirements of the final product, be it a brochure, newsletter or advertising copy. The more closely you can tailor your copy to the final "look" of the piece, the more assignments you'll get. Understanding production requirements and working well with art directors are other good ways to strengthen your value to the agency.

HOW TO GET STARTED

Getting a foot in the door in business writing can be frustrating. How can you get an assignment without experience? How can you get experience without an assignment? That dilemma applies to all kinds of writing, and the business world is no exception. That first assignment may be tough to get, but as your portfolio builds, so will your business.

The obvious place to start is in a field where you are already an expert. As I mentioned earlier, if you sell clothing during the day, look for agencies (or companies) that handle retail apparel. You know the buzzwords, you have a feel for the market and you can call on your own experience.

If you don't have this kind of experience, you really need to develop some field where you can claim specialized knowledge. Creative directors (or editors) don't have time to teach neophytes the language of their clients (or readers).

The portfolio you show creative directors doesn't have to have only (or any) business-related writing. If you've got clips of newspaper or magazine articles that prove you have a crisp, direct style, a creative director will see that immediately.

If you're a *real* beginner, and you don't have a portfolio of work to show a creative director, I'd suggest some volunteer work. Write a brochure for your church or a charitable organization, or a speech for a local organization's chairperson. Perhaps you can develop an advertisement or public service announcement for a civic club's fund-raising event. Your local public television or radio station may also be able to direct you to beginning assignments.

True, you may not get paid for this work, but it will give you a finished product to show a creative director. Psychologically, a finished product has more impact than a mere manuscript. (Also, while learning the ropes with "gratis" assignments, you'll be forced to learn the production side of the business.)

WHO NEEDS AN AGENCY?

Writing for business is easier if you live in a major market. You have direct access to the agencies with the biggest budgets, and direct access is critical. It's virtually impossible to get a new assignment without a face-to-face meeting with the creative director. Plus, the client usually wants to meet with the writer—several times.

Smaller cities have fewer agencies, and the opportunities (and budgets) are smaller, but there's still plenty of work to be had. But what if you live in Glendive, Montana—hundreds of miles from the nearest advertising or public relations agency? In that case, you've got to become your own agency. You'll have to sell your services directly to the company that needs the written material.

In your community, companies and retailers have various communications needs. Instead of marketing yourself to an agency, go directly to the client firm's owner or manager. (You can do the same thing with small businesses in the big markets.) There are many opportunities:

Advertising. Most small companies rely on newspapers or broadcast stations to develop their ads, and the final results are often amateurish. Pay attention to the advertising in your hometown. When you see something that's particularly bad, you've got an opportunity to sell your writing. The growth of cable television has opened up new markets for advertising copy, too.

Public relations. Some small companies may want to develop public relations campaigns to reach their local media but don't know how. As a writer (and one-person agency), you can help them. Even if you don't have experience, go to your library, check out a few books on the public relations business, and then develop a plan to reach a specific business in your community.

Internal communications. A manufacturing company in your community may have a continuing need for internal writing, but trouble finding an executive with the time (and ability) to do it justice. The company may need a brochure that goes to key customers, or an orientation manual for new employees, or help with special advertising copy, or a speech that the plant manager wants to give to a local civic club. These assignments won't be well publicized, but if you look around, you can find them. Your neighbor who works at the plant may be your entrée to an ongoing relationship with the company's public relations manager (who may double as personnel director).

In an isolated location, you also need to become more self-sufficient from a production standpoint. You won't have art directors and typesetters and all the other production people that an agency takes for granted. Yet, your clients will expect more than written words; they'll want a finished brochure or camera-ready copy for a newspaper ad.

The tremendous advances in desktop publishing allow you to be a true "one-stop" creative source. From your own home, you can develop attractive, professional-looking material and increase your billings at the same time. A good desktop system (and the ability to use it) can be extremely valuable.

An alternative is to hook up with a local print shop to produce the final products based on your writing. While that will reduce your overall fees, it may save a lot of hassle and result in a better-looking product. Just be sure you have someone you can rely on, because your customers will judge you by the looks of the final product. Whether you have your own desktop system or team up with a printer, you must have a complete production capability. Without it, you won't make much money in rural America.

Success in small markets may depend more on your ability to sell and produce your writing than the actual writing itself. But there's a plus side. You're your own boss, you're closer to your final product, and because you did it all, you have the pride that comes with a stronger sense of ownership.

WHAT TO CHARGE

There's no easy answer to the "how much should I charge?" question. Every situation is different — but the key factors are the marketplace, the assignment and who's doing the buying. If you're in a major market, working with big-time agencies with big-time budgets, you can command top dollar (but the competition will be greater, too). A four-page brochure might net you $1,000 or more. A speech could bring in $3,000 to $6,000. A launch guide for a new product could bring well into five figures. Detailed slide presentations and video scripts usually command the highest fees.

The biggest factor is the client's budget. Usually, the company and agency agree to an up-front budget for the entire project, with a cost broken out for the actual writing. If you're on the verge of getting an assignment and you don't know what to charge, ask around town to find out the going rate. Once you've established yourself (especially if you can get the client to ask for you by name), your price can go up. You can also charge a premium if you have technical knowledge that few other writers can claim.

In freelancing for business, you soon learn that you're really writing to a time clock. If you have a $4,000 assignment that you can complete in two drafts and a polishing, your investment of forty hours gives you a return of $100 an hour. If that same assignment takes you five drafts and several touch-ups (to say nothing of the time-draining client meetings you must endure), your hourly return quickly falls. Clients don't like to renegotiate budgets (though it does happen), and usually your first fee is what you'll take home. The more efficient you can become, the more time you'll have for other high-paying assignments.

Don't cut your price just because your time investment is reduced, however. When that creative director calls at 4 P.M. with the assignment due tomorrow, you are right where you want to be. You can still get the same fee as if you had two weeks to do the writing. True, you'll go through a pot or two of coffee that evening, but twenty-four hours later, you'll be finished (at least with the first draft).

Writing a brochure on that new ultraslim atomic widget may not be glamorous, it won't spark a lot of admiring glances at your next cocktail party, and maybe it won't carry the prestige of being published in *Esquire*. But it *will* pay your bills — and then some.

The Poet's Primer

John D. Engle, Jr.

The extent of your success in writing and publishing poetry depends largely on your attitude toward yourself and your writing. It also depends on your attitude toward learning and applying the answers to the following questions:

1. What is poetry?
2. How do I know when I've written a good poem?
3. What is the poetry market? How do I prepare to enter it?
4. What are the different kinds of poetry outlets? Where do I find them? How do I plug into them?

I hope to answer some of these questions and help you to start off with a realistic attitude so that your road to publication will be easier to travel.

BECOMING A POET, IN EVERY SENSE OF THE WORD

Your attitude is the most significant determinant of your success. It is the net with which you fish the sea of poetry. If the net is faulty, your chances of success will be seriously limited. In general, your attitude toward yourself and your writing should be positive. You must believe in yourself and your ability, and you should feel that you have something important to say and that you have a right to be heard. You are unique. You should recognize, develop and celebrate your uniqueness and sing life as you see it.

However, there is a danger in carrying this attitude too far. In spite of all the evidence to the contrary, the myth persists that poets are somehow more talented, more divinely inspired and far wiser than other people. If you believe this, you may ignore basic preparation, rules and procedures; you may have an exaggerated sense of your importance and the importance of what you write. In other words, your attitude may be unrealistic.

One of the most unrealistic attitudes fathered by the superior-poet myth is the assumption that something called *poetic license*, no doubt invented by someone too lazy to look up misspelled words and learn the rules of grammar, gives the poet rights denied to other creatures. Even a poet would never expect to ride a bicycle, drive a car or play a piano well without practical instruction and practice; but he somehow feels capable of dashing off a perfect poem with no preparation and with hardly any effort.

Actually, the basic requirements for writing and publishing poetry are rather prosaic but necessary nevertheless. Let's examine these requirements by first trying to learn what poetry is, then establishing criteria that will help us determine when we have written a good poem.

Many insist that if it doesn't rhyme, it's not poetry; others, including some editors, believe that a modern poem that rhymes is too outdated to be a poem.

In view of these conflicts, how can you make an accurate evaluation of your poetry or the poetry of others? Is there a common ground, an area of agreement, a standard of evaluation to which people of various poetic tastes and preferences can subscribe? I think there is, but you must first face the fact that rhyme and meter, or the lack of either, do not determine what is or is not a good poem; for poetry can't be measured fully on the basis of form, pattern or technique, even though such attributes are important in both writing and evaluating it.

Your attitude toward poetic form or pattern should be as realistic as your attitude toward shoes. If you were selecting shoes, you would probably examine them carefully and try on many pairs for size, comfort and style before finally choosing the pair you liked best. Even then, you would not wear the same style, color or brand the rest of your life. It is more likely that you would have several different styles of shoes for different occasions. This is how you should deal with different styles of poetry also, but you don't need to be bound to any style or styles. If you nurture your inner impulses, there will be times when you will kick off your shoes completely and allow your bare feet to print their own individual, original patterns on beaches of beauty that others have not yet discovered.

Freeing yourself from the restrictions of specific forms and techniques will keep you out of the ruts and will bring you to a better understanding of what poetry is and is not. You will find that form and technique do not make a poem any more than a shoe makes a foot. The foot is the real poem; the shoe is but the form in which the poem is wrapped. If the form doesn't fit, the poem will suffer; and to find what the poem is really like, you have to get past its wrappings.

It is true that there are poems in which form and pattern or typographical arrangement are so much a part of the poem that it is almost impossible to separate the *how* from the *what*, as John Ciardi so clearly shows in *How Does a Poem Mean?* (Houghton Mifflin). Learning this fact becomes another part of your freedom. But you also learn that mastering techniques of form is not the same as mastering the art of writing poetry — any more than making a shoe is the same as making a foot. For example, it doesn't take you long to discover that a sonnet, one of the most rigid forms of poetry, is filled with some of the greatest *and* some of the *worst* poetry ever written. Anyone of average intelligence may be taught to write a perfectly formed sonnet, but no one can guarantee that that sonnet will contain even one line of good poetry.

GIVING YOUR POEM THE ACID TEST

If form and technique are only secondary criteria for determining what a good poem is, what are the primary criteria? I believe that a reasonably workable test can be based on three fairly simple but very important questions: What does the poem say? How well is it said? Is it worth saying?

What Does the Poem Say?

Of course, the meaning or theme or idea of a poem need not be blared in italics, capitals and exclamations like the central message of a commercial. Rather, it should communicate metaphorically, symbolically, indirectly. The strength of a poem lies mainly in its metaphorical power and in its ability to imply or suggest rather than state directly; and as indicated before, the *how* of a poem may be the basic part of its *what*. But your poem should communicate *something* to the reader, if not on the first reading, at least on the second or third.

How Well Is It Said?

This question leads to the true test of poetry of whatever kind. In fact, it is a basic critical question that can be applied to all writing. If what the poem says is vague, muddled, garbled, ungrammatical, trite, or is conveyed in pompous, precious, sentimental, commonplace or obsolete language, the poem has serious faults. It does not say very well what it has to say. More often than not, the problem is grammatical. Beginning poets frequently start at the wrong end of the scale. They attempt to write great poetry before learning the basic elements of grammar — good sentence structure, punctuation, spelling and word usage.

If a poem is a hodgepodge of sentence fragments, run-on sentences, misused words, misspelled words, overworked adjectives, weak passive verbs, incorrect capitalization and punctuation or none at all; if it has an oversupply of *and*'s and *so*'s and is cluttered with the discarded bones of a dead language, such as *'tis, 'twas, thee, thou, o'er* and *e'er*; or if it is laced with trite phrases, its message will not be stated very well (even though a reader may be able to figure out the message). I am not suggesting that ungrammatical poems are always bad. I am suggesting that we should first learn the rules, then if we wish, we may break them by choice rather than by ignorance.

Is It Worth Saying?

The answer to this question will vary somewhat from poet to poet and from reader to reader. If we were perfectly honest, we could have much more "golden" silence simply by admitting that a large part of what we speak and write is really not worth much. We could all improve our word selections and our methods of presenting them through humble, honest self-evaluation. In doing this, we would find that even truth is no defense in the realm of poetry.

For example, all of us will acknowledge the truth that flowers are beautiful; but since everyone already knows this and agrees, what's the value of saying it *unless* we can say it in a new and beautiful way? What is it worth to be told in a poem that love is lovely, beauty is beautiful, sadness is sad or death is deadly? Yet thousands of poems and songs do nothing more than that, and thousands of poets write these same poems every day with little variation. As a teacher, editor, critic and contest judge, I get them by the hundreds — the sad poems and the happy poems. They say it is sad to lose a pet, child, parent, husband, wife, friend, lover; they say that having the love of a pet, child, parent, husband, wife, friend, lover is wonderful; they say that this country is great, nature is grand, God is good, and good is better than evil.

I agree with them all because what they say is true. However, it is not said very well, and although it may be worth saying for the poet and for the person for whom the poem was written, it is usually not worth saying in print for a mass audience. The paradox is that although truth is no defense for poetry, poetry must deal with truth. As Emily Dickinson advised, we must "tell all the truth, but tell it slant," which means we must tell it indirectly, figuratively, metaphorically or symbolically, with imagination, originality and honesty.

But even if you follow all the rules of good writing and your poem passes the three-question test, even if it is brilliantly original and shows great writing talent or genius, you must also follow the rules of marketing as carefully and realistically as you followed the rules of writing.

MARKETING YOUR POETRY

Many outlets for poetry are already collected and classified for you in various publications, with which you should become familiar and either own or have easy access to. These publications and your other writing materials aren't free, of course, but they are no more expensive than tools needed in other activities, such as photography and golf; besides, when you start selling your poems, all your writing expenses are tax-deductible. The publications containing market listings consist of both periodicals and books. Some or all of them may be found at libraries, bookstores or newsstands.

Poet's Market is published by Writer's Digest Books, 1507 Dana Avenue, Cincinnati, Ohio 45207. Also published at the same address are two other guides that are for writers in general, but that contain markets and other helpful material for poets. They are the monthly *Writer's Digest* and the annual *Writer's Yearbook. Writer's Digest* runs a regular column on poetry, along with up-to-date information about new poetry markets, contests, etc. *Writer's Yearbook* contains many helpful articles and ratings of the top one hundred markets.

You should subscribe to *Poets & Writers*, published six times a year by Poets & Writers, Inc., 72 Spring Street, New York, New York 10012. This publication is loaded with markets as well as information about publishing, grants, awards, contests, conferences and many other items of interest to poets.

For an almost endless supply of markets for beginners, you may wish to order the annual *International Directory of Little Magazines and Small Presses* (Dustbooks), which contains valuable information about more than five thousand market listings. It may be ordered from Dustbooks, Box 100, Paradise, California 95967, or you may be able to find it in your library.

Markets will, no doubt, be duplicated in these various sources; besides, it will take some time to collect them all. Therefore, I suggest you start with *Poet's Market*, which offers a good general introduction to all kinds of poetry outlets. Before going to any one market section, however, I urge you to read all the introductory material and other helps and suggestions; then examine the table of contents and take a slow tour through the book.

Like most beginners, you may protest the low pay of these publications and insist on finding other markets. You are free to do this, of course; but your chances of getting published in big, high-paying magazines are much slimmer because they use less poetry.

The reason most small magazines don't pay much, frequently in contributor's copies only, is that they can't afford to. They are usually run by small staffs, many of them unpaid, or by only one or two arts-dedicated people. They carry little or no advertising, and therefore, are lucky to break even financially. However, they provide a valuable proving ground for beginners; and, oddly enough, they frequently publish better poetry than is usually found in larger, commercial, high-paying publications. It is not easy to get published in these small magazines, especially the literary publications. You must be patient and persistent.

BOOKS OF POETRY

Publishing a book of poems may be possible, but it isn't likely for a beginner. As for the subsidy publishers, I urge you to steer clear of them unless you have huge amounts of money to invest in a nonprofit venture (see following article). Your best bet is to publish first in the magazines, then collect your published works into a book and see if you can find a publisher who will take it. If not, you may want to try getting it printed on your own through a local printer.

TRUE SUCCESS AS A POET

The ocean of poetry contains many shallows and depths and endless forms of life and song. You start your adventure by studying the maps and charts of those who have been there before you; then you explore the beaches, harbors, coves and beyond. But whether you walk, wade, swim, fish, sail, dive or merely sit and enjoy, you cannot lose. My wish is that you experience as much of that ocean as you feel you must, and my hope is that what I have written here will somehow help you to do it.

Safe, Sane Self-Publishing

Judson Jerome

Before I could read, I loved a book of poems written by my grandfather. It was really no more than a pamphlet, but a beautiful one, bound in soft leather, on heavy eggshell paper: *Grains of Sand*. Of the books the grownups read aloud to me, I especially liked this one because the poems were often about people in the family.

My grandfather had no more than a fifth-grade education. He worked in the oil fields, and for a time, succeeded fairly well in the rough-and-tumble oil business of Oklahoma in the 1920s. His book, and poems by my father that occasionally appeared in the Tulsa and Oklahoma City newspapers, taught me at an early age that writing poetry is an appropriate thing for a man to do. I knew, almost before I went to school, that I would be a poet.

That would never have happened if not for the noble American tradition of self-publishing. Many writers fail to realize that printers, like blacksmiths or cobblers, have shops and are looking for business. Walt Whitman was a printer himself (in fact, he not only self-published his *Leaves of Grass* but wrote a number of favorable reviews of it, under pen names, and placed them in newspapers).

There's no reason *you* can't make use of a printer's services. You might even make money, if you can sell something for more than you paid to have the printing done. But whether you make money or not, you can put your writing into a form that your friends and family can treasure, just as my grandfather did.

I am often amazed at how little most people who call themselves writers know about — or have *thought* about — publishing and printing.

When I was about ten, I got a job delivering grocery-store ads door to door in our neighborhood, being paid so much per hundred. Later I found out that my four-year-old brother was following me around, picking up a flyer, ringing the doorbell and selling the ad, if he could, to the resident for a penny.

Both of us are writers now, but he was ahead of me in training for our future careers. He saw that the point was to sell the printed sheet. You write stuff down, get someone to print it up, and then get people to buy it because they want to read what you wrote. Isn't that the business we're all in?

Where do *publishers* come into this simple process? Usually a publisher is a kind of broker. He or she will risk paying the printer and paying for distribution of your writing and splitting the profit with you. It's a very uneven split, as the publisher usually takes 90 percent of the sales price.

Publishers that advertise for manuscripts are usually *subsidy* publishers. When dealing with such firms, you pay *all* the publication costs, and you may find that you end up not owning all the books you paid to have printed. On the other hand, they handle the planning and printing for you.

But if you don't like the deal commercial publishers offer (or if they offer you none at all), and you have an adventurous spirit and the capital to risk, you *can* pay for printing and distribution yourself and keep *all* the profits. That's what self-publication means. You don't need a license or anyone's permission. You just give yourself a name, like Last Chance Press, have the printer put that name on what he prints, and you're in business.

DOLLARS AND SENSE

Of course that's what a lot of us who write don't like at all: the business end of things. However, if you know that what you write — poetry, family history, far-out experimental fiction, for instance — has little commercial value, but you want your work in print nonetheless, why not simply pay for it just as you might buy a special lens for your camera or a new pair of skis? Make it one of the expenses of your hobby, for which you expect no reward beyond your own satisfaction. If your family and friends happen to treasure the work, that's gravy. Self-publication is no more shameful than any other form of self-indulgence, and like a lot of things we pursue for our own satisfaction — arts, crafts, hobbies — it may have a high value for others as well.

But if you want to make money by writing, you must turn a good part of your thought and energy (and financial resources) to business. One writer I know, who has literally dozens of mysteries and other books of popular fiction in print, recently wrote a book on how to write. Did he send it to a publisher? No, he knew he could make more money on it by self-publishing. He was well established as a speaker and workshop leader, had plenty of public contacts, and he figured that he might as well make the investment in printing himself — and not have to split the proceeds with a publisher.

But he had a lot more interest and ability in the business end of writing than I have, than most of us have. When I consider the problems of getting a book designed, satisfactorily manufactured, advertised and (the biggest job of all) sold, I sigh and decide I'd rather make less money and let someone else do work I am neither qualified to do nor have any great interest in learning to do. I will peddle a manuscript among various publishers for a long time before I'll resort to self-publication. But I will self-publish — have done so — when I lose patience with that process or believe the book will never see print unless I pay for it.

DECISIONS, DECISIONS . . .

If you make the decision to self-publish, you have a lot of choices along the way. In the past decade, with the rise of desktop publishing, the whole business has become remarkably decentralized. Time was the publishers were all in New York or Boston. Now they are everywhere, even in small towns.

A small publisher is not likely to own or be able to buy the machinery that physically makes books. Printers do that. But you, as a self-publisher, can save money by cutting down on the number of services you ask the printer to perform, and some of these are among the costliest steps in the process.

First, of course, is composition, or *typesetting*, as we still call it (though that word by no means describes the process of getting images onto paper by computer technology). The printing process today is almost always photographic. You get the images onto clean white paper the way you want your pages to look — what's called *camera-ready* — and machines do the rest. You can take typescript into the offices of most printers, and they will be happy to prepare it for the camera for you, for a price. But today it's remarkably easy to save money (and exercise more control) by doing much of that yourself.

The first thing a reader notices about a page that has been typeset is its proportional spacing, though the reader may not recognize that term. Typewriting looks like typewriting, as do most products of word processing, because the letters are not proportionally spaced. On a typewriter or ordinary word-processing program, all the letters and symbols are the same width. It takes as much of the page to print (.) or *i* as it does *m*. A big step toward self-publishing, if you want to turn out pages that look like type and not typewriting, is to acquire one of the many word-processing fonts available that are in proportional spacing.

Then again, when I was working on a novel published by Applezaba Press, this small press asked for the book on disk. I sent it to them in WordPerfect 5.1, and in proportional spacing (Dutch 12 point, available for WordPerfect from Bitstream), and the publisher printed it out just as I sent it to him. Upon seeing the finished product, I began to realize how different in many details type was from even sophisticated word processing. For example, for a dash, what is called an "em dash" in printing, I used two hyphens, as we are taught to do in typing class.

That's fine in a letter, but it looks amateurish in a book. A typewriter or word-processing quotation marks are the same for the beginning and end of a quote (″), whereas printing uses inverted commas: (" "). The difference is most noticeable when you come to single quotes, for which typing uses an apostrophe ('). While the little symbols for a double quotation mark are neutral, up and down, the apostrophe definitely looks like the closing, but not the opening of a quotation. You need (' '). We were taught in typing to leave two spaces after a period or at the end of a sentence. Printing uses one. (I saved three whole pages on a 250-page manuscript by doing a mass hunt-and-replace, changing two spaces to one.) All these special characters can be generated by many word-processing programs, but you have to learn how to make them do it.

In other words, self-publishing is a matter of degree. You can turn out a page that looks very much like a typeset page or one that approximates that "ideal" to one degree or another. It all depends on how much you're willing to invest in your word-processing system, how much you want the printer to do, and how "professional" you want the final job to look.

I put "ideal" and "professional" in quotation marks to imply "so-called." In my opinion, the professional ideal is sometimes silly, and sometimes worse than that. For example, most professionally printed books use right-hand justification. There is no reason that lines should all come out even on the right margin, and studies have shown that they are harder to read when they do. We print books in that style because the Romans learned from the Arabs that that was the way to do it. It makes sense in Arabic, which begins at the right margin and goes left, but it made no sense in Latin; yet in the early scriptoriums, where one slave dictated and a roomful of slaves took down his words and turned them into a book, they carefully spaced their words to come out even on the right. In the Middle Ages, monks making books in lofty carrels imitated the Roman practice, because that was the civilized thing to do. And when Gutenberg and others invented moveable type, they went to great pains to space between words with tiny, blank slugs — called *ems* and *ens* — so that their manufactured books would look handmade, on the same principle that a shoe manufacturer might want to use a machine to turn out sandals that appeared to be hand-crafted.

Ems and ens worked well enough while people set type by hand, but there are no such spaces on a typewriter, of course. And when typesetting began to be mechanized by computers, a great deal of extra work went into making right-hand justification possible. Now, most word-processing programs have a setting that enables you to justify on the right. Don't use it when preparing manuscripts for submission. Most editors *hate* it, because it makes the spacing between words all uneven, so they have a hard time telling whether there is an extra space in the manuscript that should be removed or if they are just looking at a peculiarity caused by crude justification. Besides, justified manuscripts are harder to read.

Nonetheless, thanks to great technological ingenuity and as a result of untold expense, most camera-ready copy is justified. If that's how you want your book to look, you do it that way. That's what I call silly or worse, but it is the professional ideal.

DESKTOP PUBLISHING

If you're really serious about doing your own publishing, you *can* eliminate the uneven spacing that results when most word-processing texts are justified. Special programs available for desktop publishing (QuarkXpress, PageMaker and Ventura Publishing are among the most popular) enable you to use many more refinements than simple word processing makes possible. For example, not only can you control, down to several decimal places, the font size, but you can control the *leading* (rhymes with *bedding*), the blank space between lines. There is essentially no difference between a text prepared by these programs and one that is typeset by hand. And if you're thinking of self-publishing a book that you expect to market widely, and to have reviewed, you need such a desktop-publishing package to do the job. These programs are neither cheap nor easy to learn, but they virtually turn your computer into a print shop. (Once you get a book in camera-ready state with one of these programs, the process of actually printing, collating, trimming and binding the pages is a relatively small part of the overall expense.)

PEDDLE OR PERISH

Once you set cartons of printed books in your basement, what do you do with them? Well, *that's* the real problem in self-publishing. When I started my own Trunk Press back in the 1970s, an editor with a large publishing firm observed, "Printing a book is easy. It's getting rid of it that's hard." She was right.

There are, of course, spectacular stories of self-publishing success. A book telling amateurs about Volkswagen repair, written and published on a commune in the 1960s, became a nationwide bestseller, and the group that produced it is now a mainline publisher of a wide range of books. One couple has been living off their book on sailing for many years. They pull into a harbor now and then to send off revisions to the printer and take care of business, and off they go before the wind again.

But these success stories always concern nonfiction books, more specifically how-to books. If you know how to do something and can explain it colorfully and clearly, and have a head for business, you might make a financial success of self-publishing. For one thing, if you're deeply involved in a specialized activity (making reproductions of muzzle-loading guns, for instance) you probably already know how to reach your probable audience — where to buy ads, etc. Such books can succeed by mail order.

Other nonfiction titles, especially on very specialized topics, can similarly be marketed by mail order. I knew of one on divorce laws in a particular state that did very well over a period of many years. Enough people needed to know about such things and found it hard to get information collected in one place. But self-publishing is no way to bring fiction or poetry or philosophy or general social commentary — the normal books sold through the book-publishing trade — to public attention. If you buy a how-to book on piano tuning, it may not be very well written and may have some errors, but there's a good chance, even if you buy it from an ad, that you'll learn something you didn't know about piano tuning. But would you buy a book from an ad alone, without having read reviews, without having any expert assessment available, without having heard of the author, if it was about the political balance in the Middle East? How about a novel about the disintegration of the marriage of a depressed librarian in a small Sussex town? How about a book of poetry that the author promises will tell you the meaning of life? Well, you may be an exception, but generally ads for such books don't sell them.

Once you become a publisher, or even start the process of becoming one, you'll find that you are a member of a club. In fact, one of the first things you're likely to want to do is join COSMEP, the international association of independent publishers (Box 420703, San Francisco, California 94142). Send an SASE for its brochure. The association publishes a newsletter and has a wide range of publications and activities to support the work of small presses. You'll also find electronic bulletin boards linking members interested in desktop publishing, distribution and other matters that are now in your professional bailiwick. In time, you'll figure out which are the book distributors that might consider taking you on as a client — and handling your sales to bookstores and other outlets.

Another thing you'll quickly discover, if you strike out on your own as a publisher, is why books cost so much these days. And you may discover, too, why writers find it so hard to find a publisher to invest in their work. Once you've risked some of your own money on making a book of your own a success, ask yourself if you'd be willing to risk it again on someone else's writing.

IV.

Moving Up the Ladder to the Big Time

Writer Meets Editor

James Morgan

Believe it or not, lots of people think editors and writers are one and the same. I once presided over a chamber of commerce publication during a time in my life I now refer to vaguely as "when I edited a city mag," and even my boss didn't understand the difference; to him, a writer was someone he could pay peanuts whenever his services were needed, while an editor was someone he had to pay peanuts *all the time*. And for what? All he saw in the magazine was the writing.

One day I overheard him asking his henchman, "Can't we run this magazine without an editor?" To which I eventually replied, "Without *this* editor you can," and split.

No, editors and writers aren't the same. They're mutant species of the same genus, of course, and they exhibit certain vestigial similarities; but they're really two different animals. A magazine needs both kinds, and each kind needs the other. And when the relationship works the way it's supposed to, it's tremendously rewarding for both.

How, exactly, does that relationship work? Several metaphors come to mind: the editor as headquarters general (I visualize someone kind and Ike-like, though you writers are likely to conjure up Brando in *Apocalypse Now*), with the writer as front-line soldier. Or the editor as baseball manager, with the writer as designated hitter. Or how about this: the editor as circus ringmaster, the writer as high-wire artist. There's something about the circus metaphor that's perversely appropriate.

But metaphors have their limits, don't they? Really, the best way to understand how editors and writers are supposed to work with one another is to follow them through the process that links them — in this case, the preparation of a magazine article. Every project is different, of course — that's part of what makes our business stimulating — and every editor-writer relationship is different, too. But the process itself is pretty much the same every time. By seeing how at least one experienced editor thinks it *ought* to go, maybe you can figure out why it sometimes doesn't go that way for you. Then, next time, maybe it will.

STEP 1: THE ASSIGNMENT

It all starts with an idea. If the idea comes from the writer in the form of a query, the editor generally makes a few suggestions and then dispatches the writer to go out and seek whatever slice of Truth the two of them have decided they're after. But if the idea comes from the editor, the process is a little more complex.

In terms of the editor-writer relationship, the two most important things are that (1) the editor choose the right writer for the job and (2) the editor explain what the heck he wants the writer to do.

You may think I'm insulting you by offering such obvious information. The fact is, though, you experienced writers know that many editors don't have any real idea of what they want until they've seen samples of what they *don't* want. Of course, since this is a partnership, it's as much the writer's fault as it is the editor's: As a writer, you shouldn't accept an assignment unless you're comfortable that you and the editor are working on the same story.

All of which is why I believe so strongly in the assignment letter: Aside from formalizing the basic information about length, fee and deadline, it gives the editor a chance to think and rethink the concept, to word it just right; it also gives the writer something to refer to from time to time when writing the piece. And finally, it provides a point of reference if there's still some disagreement over whether the finished piece accomplished what it was supposed to do.

But we're getting ahead of ourselves. The first point I mentioned in regard to the editor-writer relationship was the editor's choice of the right writer. Obviously, there's a lot of subjectivity involved in that choice, and I think that's fine: The editor has a right to pick someone he feels comfortable working with — someone he feels not only can do the job, but also can bring something special to it.

When I was at *Playboy*, we decided to assign an article on David Duke, then the young, slick, button-downed, silver-tongued leader of what he called a "new" Ku Klux Klan. While there are Klansmen everywhere, we felt that the piece needed a Southern writer, someone to whom Duke's boiling racist blood might at least be viscerally understandable. We didn't want someone who *agreed* with him, mind you, but someone who might bring a sense of complexity to the piece. And since the Klan isn't the same as the D.A.R., we also wanted someone who wasn't afraid to take that proverbial walk on the wild side.

Others had suggested articles on the Klan, but the writer we came up with was Harry Crews, the earthy, eloquent Georgia native who teaches English at the University of Florida between novels and articles on such subjects as bulldog fighting, truckers and traveling carnivals — all of which sounded to us like perfect practice for this assignment.

More about that later. We gave Crews the Klan assignment because it fit his experience. But if an editor simply relies on a writer's past assignments in order to give him more of the same, then writer, editor and magazine will all get stale. One of the most inspired matchups I've ever been associated with also happened during my *Playboy* days. One of the editors had the brilliant notion of sending a New York street kid to cover the much-venerated (in the South) Alabama football coach Bear Bryant. The writer was Richard Price, who by then had written a couple of tough novels about street gangs and has since won an Oscar for his gritty screenplay for *The Color of Money*; Price wasn't interested in football particularly, and he didn't know a thing about the South; but he was interested in power and winning with all the heart a New York street kid can muster, and he came back with an irreverent yet sensitive piece on one of football's greats.

So the choice of writer is very important — but that's only the beginning of the editor's job. After he's picked the writer, and before the writer gets out on his own, the editor must do everything he can to make sure he and his writer understand each other. Virtually no law of science can ensure that two human beings will actually *communicate* so that each understands what the other means. And sometimes both parties let this process get complicated by the presence of a third party — the agent.

Not all writers have agents of course, and not all writers who have agents use them for magazine pieces. But when an agent is involved, his job is primarily to make sure the writer gets as much money as possible. The agents are the bankers of this business, the scorekeepers, the bill collectors, the dealers, the readers and writers of small print. Essence and Meaning are languages they seldom speak, at least with editors. For many writers, the agent lifts the unpleasant burden of discussing money so the writer can concentrate on the sometimes-unpleasant-but-preferable task of writing.

But in no case should either editor or writer allow the agent to be the total communications conduit. Talk Money with the agent, but talk Meaning with each other. One of the joys — and ironies — of this business is that while it *is* a business, its success depends on the effectiveness of the personal, human communication. To be effective businesspeople, editors and writers have to be human first, business-people second.

And to be human means to understand human frailty — which raises the subject of procrastination. Some editors think they're doing the writers a favor by leaving the deadline open. I think most people, editors included, work better with a definite deadline. Whose rule is that about a job expanding to fill the time available? An assignment without a deadline can become a psychological albatross for the writer: As you writers know, it's hard as hell to sit alone in a room and run your soul through a word processor, and there's a tendency to hold on to your soul until somebody says you have to bare it. Besides, an editor who doesn't set deadlines can't very well do the rest of his job — planning timely issues, working out a balanced mix, that sort of stuff. Chaos may be the natural order of things in this business, and you're more likely to remain sane if you realize you can't change that. But you've still got to try.

STEP 2: THE WAITING GAME

Harry Crews's piece on the Klan was due, but instead of a manuscript, a short letter and a Polaroid color photograph landed in my in-box. The letter was apologetic: Crews is a proud man, and he had never missed a deadline before. But there had been a little trouble, he said, and he was laid up a bit. The attached photograph was to show me what a man's stomach looks like after it's been mauled with a spring-loaded blackjack.

When I called Crews, he apologized again for missing the deadline and asked whether I still wanted him to finish the piece. Of *course* I did, but that was beside the point: How was he? Was he taking care of himself? As it turns out he was, in his way, and we went on with the prosaic details of discussing the piece and setting a new deadline. When the article was in, Crews wrote me a note thanking me for being understanding.

Understanding. It's something an editor must be, especially once that assignment is made and the writer is out in the trenches. Out there any number of things can go wrong, and the editor must stand by to act as monitor, cheerleader, big brother, best friend, devil's advocate, drill sergeant, banker, marriage counselor, travel agent, coach and shrink. Any editor in his right mind would've been understanding in Crews's case, but not every situation is that clear-cut. I once called a writer for days trying to find out where her manuscript was. When I finally got through, her daughter answered the phone and said, "She can't talk right now — she's meditating." Right about then I was tempted to give her a new mantra: *unemployed*. But her copy arrived the next day, and it was brilliant, as usual. (You writers should bear this in mind: If you insist on being pains in the ass, you better make sure you're worth it.)

I could go on for pages about the various cases in which editors are called on to be understanding about the situations writers have put them in — or vice versa, depending on who's telling the story. The point is, being understanding is the idea; being responsive is the absolute minimum. Once an editor gets an assignment made, he goes on to deal with other writers, other assignments, and each one has its own litany of facts, fees, logistics and nuances. The editor is a busy person, but he shouldn't ever get so busy that he can't return his writers' phone calls, answer their letters, see that their expense checks are sent and answer their questions. There are many thrills to being an editor, but there's also a heap of drudgery, and an editor must be able to work that drudgery into his day. Mainly, he's got to figure out his priorities, just like any other manager must do, and that means remembering that those writers he's already assigned are more important, maybe, than the new ones he's working on. He's got to look to the future, but if he doesn't take care of today there won't be any future left when he gets there.

Writers are the people editors call to solve the editors' problems, so it's only fair that editors be the ones writers call to solve their problems. There's no guarantee, of course, that the editor will be of any *real* help at this stage, but sometimes that's OK. At this point, the writer who's wrestling with how to organize the piece, for example, is satisfied to hear the editor say: "Damn, I don't know. Let's talk about it." And maybe that's all it'll take — a return to that one-on-one human relationship that existed before the assignment letter went out.

Something both editors and writers should remember, though, is that each of you is well served by a writer who, having dug into the story a bit, calls the editor and says, "Hey, the story *isn't* the way you see it — isn't the way we discussed it beforehand." I mention this because I've stressed so much the editor's responsibility to convey *his* concept, *his* feelings about the piece he's assigning. But in the end, the writer is the one on the front line, the one who senses the shape of the story first, the one who has to invest his time and energies writing the piece. If he feels that it's nowhere near the story the editor is expecting, he'd better say so, and right now.

STEP 3: THE MANUSCRIPT

I can't remember an article ever being as good in actuality as it was in my mind the moment I assigned it.

There's a reason for that, of course: In my mind I hadn't encountered any obstacles, hadn't gone so far as to think in lines, or even paragraphs; I hadn't crafted a lead or an ending, no hard-hitting images, no drop-dead dialogue. All I had was a vague *feeling*, a sense of tone. That, coupled with my reason for assigning the piece, had made the article a great read — mentally.

But even in the magazine world, where some egos need a wide-load sign and larger-than-life dreams careen through the halls, sooner or later you must deal with reality, the first recorded stage in the magazine process. Reality shrinks the farther you go toward actual publication: The writer grapples with the infinity of the initial concept, eventually pinning a slice of it to paper; the editor deals with a little less — his own earlier preconceptions and purposes balanced against what the writer finally gives him; the art director considers the editor's ideas and comes up with something he must contain on a few pages; the keyliner measures the world in picas.

As soon as the piece comes in, the editor shifts an internal gear or two and glides from his conceptualizer role to that of synthesizer. No more blue skies, no Technicolor visions. Now he's got to balance his expectations against the actual manuscript, mix in the fact-checker's suggestions, weigh alterations asked for by the legal department, occasionally even trim for the prosaic-yet-profound purpose of fitting the article into the magazine. (I sometimes think of the assignment stage as the period of promise — and everything afterward as the period of *com*promise.)

Now comes the critical moment. Just picture where the editor and writer are sitting in this emotion-charged game. All along, the editor has put the pressure on the writer, challenged him to perform, exhorted him, cajoled. Now it's the editor's turn to play offense, to get off the sidelines and show his stuff: his judgment, his critical acumen, his ability to focus, to select, to figure out and diplomatically convey to the writer what the hell to *do* with all those pages sitting in the editor's in-box stained with the writer's blood. It's relatively easy to have a good idea, but it's not so easy to know how to move it, through other people, from concept to printed page.

And the writer? He's tense. Writing is a potentially humiliating experience, a hero-or-goat risk venture, and the writer wants to know — at the same time that he doesn't — what the editor's verdict is.

I prefer to give a piece a couple of readings and then respond to the writer by mail. With a letter, the editor gets to thin out and organize what he has to say; he gets to soften his criticisms with a few strokes; and the writer can read the letter several times, so that the editor's words have a chance to sink in, and maybe make sense, before the writer responds. I generally suggest that the writer give me a call after he's had a chance to read and think about my comments.

If a writer's smart, he'll give the editor a couple of weeks before calling to see what the editor thinks of the piece. And if the editor's smart, he won't wait for the writer to call. That's a lesson I think about every time I recall an episode I endured with a writer I'll call Ballard.

I was working late one afternoon and made the mistake of picking up on an after-hours phone call. "Morgan?" said the voice. "This is Ballard. What did you think about my piece?" I had received his article the day before.

"Hey, man," I said, feeling a little like Dr. Faustus taking an un-screened call from Mephistopheles. The fact was, I *had* read his piece, and I liked it — but there was something a little off about it, something vague, possibly structural. I just hadn't set aside the time to figure out what the problem was, and I didn't want to commit to buying it just yet.

"Well?" he said. I could hear him puffing on a cigarette like a man getting ready to go to war.

"Well," I said, "I like the piece . . . but there seems to be something slightly wrong with it that I haven't been able to put my finger on. Something structural, maybe."

"You don't like it," he said, lighting up again.

"Yeah, I *do*," I said. "It's just that — "

"Well, you can just put that SOB in an envelope and ship it right back. I don't *deserve* this kind of treatment."

At which point *I* got mad and we went on from there. I apologized to him for not getting in touch within twenty-four hours (I think my sarcasm went right past him), but told him I wasn't shipping the piece back until I got around to figuring out what it needed, which I did within the next day or so. I sent him a letter with my comments, and he thought they were on target; we then made the necessary corrections. Later, he told me he had just gotten nervous and impatient and decided he couldn't wait any longer.

Oh, one other thing: Before calling, he had fortified himself with fourteen beers.

There's a lot about the editor-writer relationship that can drive either party to drink, and at no time does the process get more tense than at this stage, this twilight zone between the time the writer has turned in the manuscript and the editor has uttered the five words a freelancer never tires of hearing: "What's your Social Security number?" That means a check will soon be on its way.

But even after that, the road is littered with obstacles. The editor will put a pencil to the piece, of course, and will send galleys off for the writer to review. If the main revisions have already been done by this point — as they certainly should've been — there should be few surprises. But I think a few words about this process are in order, for editors as well as writers.

Editing *isn't* rewriting. Editing *isn't* homogenizing a writer's style so that the only thing different from one article to another is the subject. Forget for a moment that the editor holds the power of the purse strings; that kind of power is weak in comparison to the power of good editing. Because editing is diplomacy, and diplomacy is getting what you want by convincing others that what you want is right. Diplomacy is tact, taste and timing. And compromise.

Richard Price wrote his piece on Bear Bryant about twice as long as it appeared in the magazine — which is to say, a lot longer than we asked for. He was apprehensive when his editor told him it was going to have to be cut, but he was willing to wait and see. The editor made the cuts, taking out large chunks at a time. When you cut, you usually have to rework the transitions so the paragraphs fit together again. The editor sent the revisions to Price, along with a suggestion for a new ending. Price rewrote some of the transitions and tried for another ending, which *we* then didn't like. We reorganized a paragraph or two to shape yet another ending — which Price didn't like. Finally, Price came up with still another ending that all of us could live with. Fortunately, Bear Bryant never suffered such a working over on the playing field.

It's all part of the give-and-take of the editor-writer alliance. Ours is a very personal, private work that's eventually displayed in public, and we have to be careful of — and thankful for — each other. *Playboy* couldn't really have demanded that Price accept our ending of his piece — after all, we hired him to give us his insights into Bear Bryant, and his name goes on the piece. But the magazine's name goes *over* the piece, and if we had felt, say, that the ending he wanted was somehow an embarrassment to the magazine (we didn't, by the way), we probably would've had to reject the article. Seldom does it come to that if it's gone as far as this project had, because by that time both parties have a real stake in making the thing work. The art of compromise doesn't mean simply rolling over; it means knowing how far to roll before you draw the line.

All editors have been guilty of drawing it too early. When Norman Mailer wanted more space than usual between the lines of *Playboy*'s excerpt of *The Executioner's Song* (Random House), Mailer's gripping story of Gary Gilmore, I refused; fortunately, editorial director Arthur Kretchmer decided it was worth having a look at the type before we said no, and we wound up salvaging a blockbuster.

But sometimes we don't draw the line soon enough. I once endured the ravings of a wonderful writer who, having reviewed the galleys of his article, suddenly turned into an insufferable prima donna: *We had cut some commas, and he wanted them put back.* Our copy chief had marked them to be omitted, and I had approved the cuts. All professional magazines have style books that cover everything from whether to spell *okay* "O.K." or "okay" (here it's "OK"), or what to do in the case of serial commas. It's the copy editor's job to ride herd on style, so the editor of an individual article is usually caught between a rock (the copy editor) and a hard place (the writer). The editor must try to please both. I do believe, however, that the editor on the piece, not the copy editor, should have the final say on how a piece should run. (Especially if *I'm* the editor on the piece!)

In the case of the comma prima donna, I eventually agreed to go over the galleys with him and hear the case for keeping each damn comma. It took a lot of conversations, a lot of hours, and it underscored for me what an ego-intensive business this is, what hard questions there are to answer. All the writer has is his words and how he's strung them together; I understand that. I also understand that if *every* writer went to the mat over every comma, we'd never get out a magazine.

I was going to end this piece with the preceding paragraph, but that didn't seem quite fair: The example wasn't typical, really, of the editor-writer relationship. It was just a glimpse, for the purpose of example, at how minuscule the points of discussion can be, and how vast the understanding and sensitivity must be, then, each side for the other. I'm sure writers tell just as many such stories about editors.

But editors, because they hold the purse strings, generally get the last word, and I thought I might change that here. Because a friend of mine, a writer who was once an editor, inscribed his first book to me with words that capture something basic about this marriage of talents that is the editor-writer relationship. On the surface he's talking economics, a subject editors and writers often discuss. But between the lines, there's more: a truth, maybe, about the temperaments of each side, and a hint at each one's occasional yearnings, when his own chosen pressures get too fierce, to switch places with the other:

> Writin' ain't as bad
> as goin' to work.
> It also ain't as good
> as makin' a living.

At the time, I thought he was writing about himself. Now I know he was talking about all of us.

Turning Local Into National Magazine Article Sales

Judy Keene

As a beginning freelancer, I followed the same well-worn path toward publication trod by many writers before me — the local and regional markets. *Hoosier Outdoors* bought several camping pieces, and I wrote articles on Indiana people and events for the Sunday magazine sections of the Indianapolis *Star* and the South Bend *Tribune*. Eventually, I began to write in-depth features for *Indianapolis Magazine*.

These publications offered an excellent training ground, but it wasn't long before I yearned to stretch beyond these self-imposed geographical boundaries. I began to query publications in other states, and my list of credits soon grew to include, first, regional publications outside my own area, and then, such markets as *Kiwanis* magazine, *The Elks Magazine* and *American Way*. Although I was now reaching a much wider audience, my articles still were usually based on a local person, organization or event.

There was still another bridge to cross — the one that would take me to a national audience with a story that was truly national in scope. How gratifying it would be, I fantasized, to pass the magazines displayed at the supermarket checkout and know that my own words were tucked inside, available to literally millions of readers!

At about the same time I had reached this point in my professional life, my personal life was revolving around a friend in the throes of a bitter divorce. She called me constantly, seeking advice and comfort, and I was having a difficult time knowing how to help.

A writer friend of mine recently said that the problem with being a freelancer was that never again could she just live her life — that every situation was now a potential article. This was exactly the case in my situation. I knew my concern was far from unique and that nearly every woman from Maine to California had been in similar shoes at one time or another. In short, I knew that counseling a friend was an article idea with wide enough appeal for a major national publication.

Some of the techniques I needed now were the same as I had used for the smaller publications. First, I studied the various women's magazines to determine where my idea was most likely to find a home. I listed them in the order that I would query them, putting *Glamour* in the number-one position. Upon analyzing several issues of that magazine, I found that their self-help articles relied heavily on anecdotes and professional guidance. This, then, would be the format I would follow — both in my query, and hopefully, in the subsequent article.

I contacted a family counselor in nearby Indianapolis and talked to friends about their experiences with helping a friend through a crisis. From what I learned, I wrote the query.

Within a few days, an editor at *Glamour* called to tell me they did indeed want the article and to give me some basic direction concerning such things as word length. She reminded me that the article must be national in scope and promised that a contract would soon be on its way.

By the time the call ended, I already had visions of newsstands filled with my byline. The writing I now had to do, however, presented some challenges I had never met before; namely, where to find individuals throughout the country who would talk to me about this rather personal subject.

I began by interviewing my local expert at length. She not only answered all my questions on the subject, but she also provided names of her counterparts from West Palm Beach to Lexington to Colorado Springs. These were individuals well known in their field, and while some were known to her only by reputation, others were friends.

To each person on my list, I sent an identical letter describing what I was writing for *Glamour* and explaining how I had gotten the person's name. I wrote that I would be calling their offices the following week, and, should they be willing to help, I would need from their secretaries a time convenient for a telephone interview.

All my sources were not only willing, but also eager, to cooperate. They freely gave me their very valuable time, and not only answered my questions but pointed me toward additional areas I might explore.

To help illustrate the points made by these experts, I needed individuals who had acted as counselors for friends. While I had used my friends Karen and Sandy in my query, I felt I would get the best material by talking to strangers — preferably strangers scattered across the United States.

I wrote another letter, once again describing my project, to several friends now living in other states. I asked them to put me in contact with young women who would be willing to share their experiences with me, and once more the response was overwhelmingly positive. A cousin in California led me to her friends, and a college friend now living in Colorado lined up several of her employees to talk to me. Another friend gave me the name of a young minister's wife in Florida whose story was perfect for my lead.

Had this approach not worked, my alternative would have been to use the national directory of Women in Communications, Inc., of which I am a member, to contact fellow members throughout the country. While it was unnecessary to do this for the *Glamour* article, it is an approach I will use in the future. In instances like this one, membership in a professional organization can be a real advantage for a freelancer.

After many phone calls, I had a mountain of notes to transcribe and organize, but my interviewees — none of whom I had known before our conversations — were so open and helpful that the article fell together easily.

The article was mailed a few days prior to my contractual deadline, and during the next several weeks, I was alternately sure the editors were going to be amazed at the manuscript's total perfection and absolutely certain they were going to hate every word.

About six weeks passed before I learned their reaction was somewhere between these two extremes. The editor I had first spoken with called to say the manuscript was "good," but "not yet exactly right." She apologized for her vagueness, but said she really couldn't give me specific directions toward the remedy, although she tried in general terms to explain what was wrong.

For several days, I was at a standstill. Because my writing for smaller publications had always been accepted as it was written, I felt I had been struck a real blow. Who was I kidding, I scolded myself, to think that I could write for the big time? How was I going to face the rejection? And why, oh why, had I mentioned the assignment to so many friends?

Finally, I sat down to the task. I scored my transcribed notes, marking unused material with a crayon and deciding which of it would be included in the revision. I transferred some material from near the end of the manuscript to the beginning, searched for imbalance, scruti-nized for inconsistencies. I retyped the manuscript and mailed it, con-vinced that even if it still was not right, it was the best I could do.

Happily, the second try was deemed to be "much improved," and within two weeks, the check arrived. A subsequent conversation with the editor at a writers' conference convinced me that four, five or even six revisions were not uncommon and that I should be proud that only one had been requested. When the article, "When a Friend Needs Your Help," was published in the July 1983 *Glamour*, I felt that I had come to another milestone in my freelancing career. I had crossed the bridge to a major national market, and I had learned to expand a story to make it suitable for a widespread audience. Best of all, I could look at my supermarket newsstand with a new feeling of confidence—I know it will contain my work again!

Are There Hidden Sales in Your Files?

Mansfield Latimer

True, nothing is as powerful as an idea whose time has come, but I have discovered a more important truth: Nothing is as salable as an article or story whose time has come.

I discovered this while filing the copy of an article I had just written. I noticed a short story listed on an adjoining folder: "Second Chance." At the time I had written the story, years earlier, I had thought it was good. But after receiving a dozen rejection slips, I had decided it must not be as good as I had thought — although there were a number of encouraging letters from editors, who had rejected it for various reasons not related to the story. Reluctantly, I had filed it away.

Now, I reread the story, and my faith in it was renewed. Without making any changes, I mailed it to *Columbia*. A month later, the editor sent me a letter that began with the favorite words of all writers: "We have selected your short story, 'Second Chance,' for use in *Columbia*. A check for $300 for the story will be coming to you shortly."

Inspired, I wondered if there might be other stories or articles in my file that could now be sold — even though they had been previously rejected. I discovered a number of manuscripts that I believed could be sold. Most needed a little work — a new title, a new lead, or sometimes a complete rewrite. Working with those stories, I developed a checklist of nine ways to salvage previously unsold articles. Use them to mine gold from *your* files.

NINE KEYS TO SALES

1. Review each article in the light of changing conditions and trends. Is the article now relevant?

For example: I found a short article on insulating a house that I had written long before energy conservation was the urgent concern it is today. I wrote a new lead that emphasized the savings to be gained by insulating. I sold the modernized article to *Rural Georgia Electric Magazine.*

2. Magazines change their editorial policies, so study what is currently being published. A magazine may now be in the market for the type of articles its editors formerly rejected.

For example: Through market study, I noticed that National Research Bureau was printing the type of articles the editors had previously rejected. I sent them an article from my file titled "If I'm Smarter Than Joe, Why Didn't I Get the Promotion?", an article the magazine wouldn't have used in the past. This time, the submission brought a check.

3. Don't hesitate to resubmit an article. The magazine may have a new editor — or the same one may now like your article.

For example: I had written a specialized tennis article that was suitable for a limited number of magazines. I did not know of any new markets and was on the verge of refiling the article when I decided to send it back to some of the magazines that had previously rejected it. It had been a number of years since the original mailing, and some of those magazines had new editors. If the magazine didn't have a new editor, I reasoned that the old editor probably would not remember the article. (After all, it hadn't impressed him on the original mailing.) I mailed the article to *Tennis.* Results: another sale and a check for $200.

4. Sometimes a new title will revive an article.

For example: I once wrote an article I titled "Losers and Winners." It didn't sell. When I pulled it from my file, I realized that the title was negative. Who wants to read about losers? I changed it to the more positive "We Can All Be Winners" and it sold to *High Adventure.*

5. Most writers have received rejection slips with a note reading: "Sorry, but we recently ran a similar article." When you receive such a note, consider it an invitation to submit the article at a later date. The magazine ran that type of article once — chances are it will use another like it. Why not *your* article?

For example: In a situation like this, following up on my original query to *Office Supervisor's Bulletin* resulted in the eventual sale of "How to Overcome Your Reading Problems" and a check for $100.

6. Don't overlook articles that you have sold once. Maybe it's time to update and rewrite. Another sale may result.

For example: I rewrote and updated a previously sold article on marriage, then I sold it to *Family Life Today*.

7. New magazines are being published every month. Study the market section of *Writer's Digest* for information about these new magazines (and changes in old magazines). You may find that some of these new magazines are looking for the type of article you have already written.

For example: *Supermarket Shopper*, a new market for me, bought my previously written and unsold article "You Have Been Ripped Off."

8. As you read magazines and newspapers, be alert for news items that may strengthen articles you have already written.

For example: I recently noticed two separate newspaper articles about dogs killing people. These items reminded me of an article I had written about that subject, so I wrote a new lead that incorporated these stories from the newspaper. *Dog Fancy* magazine bought the freshened story for $60.

9. Consider the possibility that your article or story didn't sell because it wasn't professionally written. You are now a better writer than you were ten years ago. If the article idea is good, maybe it will sell now if you rewrite it. Remember, you have already done the research.

For example: I rewrote an unsold article about children and money and sent it to *Living With Children*. Results: a sale and a check.

The process of salvaging salable material from your files is a little like editorial alchemy — turning unsold lead into golden, salable prose. But unlike alchemy of old, no magic is needed. Just some polishing, and some hard work. Mine your files, and find your own gold.

Your Passport to Worldwide Sales

Michael H. Sedge

How well do your words travel? Are you as popular with editors in London, Sydney and Tokyo as you are in your hometown?

As an experienced writer selling articles around the world, I know that most American writers miss out on the potential wealth of marketing to publications outside their own country. It's a costly omission: Magazines overseas regularly purchase foreign-language rights or slightly rewritten versions of articles already published in the United States and Canada. For instance, I've collected $1,000 by selling Norwegian rights to a scuba diving article that I'd already sold to *Oceans* in the United States.

To prepare your words for travel and to be successful at foreign sales doesn't require much special knowledge beyond *thinking internationally*. You must learn to put yourself in the shoes of Germans, Australians and Japanese, for instance, as you decide which of your articles can travel to these countries.

Luckily, foreign readers are often interested in the same subjects as U.S. audiences. Modern communications have shrunk the globe, and everyone watches the United States closely. Foreign news broadcasts regularly cover Washington and U.S. affairs. As a result, U.S. business and politics are hot topics for many foreign periodicals and newspapers.

Because many foreign television networks purchase their programs from the United States, celebrity articles or anything dealing with *Roseanne, Murphy Brown, General Hospital* and other well-known series are always in demand. Movie, music and (to a lesser degree) book personality pieces also fall into this most-wanted category. I once collected $1,100 by selling a feature on Stephen King to magazines in West Germany, Italy, India and Sweden.

Travel magazines feature American destinations. And in-flight magazines are as lucrative a market elsewhere as they are in North America. I've sold general interest pieces covering topics ranging from jellyfish to macro photography in this market.

Magazines for women reflect similar problems, dreams and desires, whether they're published in New Zealand or Singapore or New York. Medicine, family problems, cosmetics and fashions are among the common topics.

And as the popularity of American sports spreads, so does the demand for good interviews and general sports articles. That goes for almost all sports — from football, baseball and basketball to tennis, boxing, auto racing, gymnastics, track and field, and golf.

Not all topics that sell in the United States or Canada will sell equally well overseas, of course. A topic that appeals to New Yorkers, for example, may be taboo in Arab nations. This is when it's helpful to know about the histories, habits, cultures and governments of the countries you wish to sell in.

I learned this lesson the hard way. I had sold "The Smoke of Kings" in the United States, and I considered this feature on the world's finest tobacco products an easy foreign sale. To my amazement, most of my proposals came back rejected. Two editors explained that government regulations in their countries forbid the promotion of tobacco products in any way. Obviously, I did not know my markets as well as I thought.

One way to become a quick expert on any country is to read the "Background Notes" published by the U.S. Department of State. These short fact sheets cover every nation of the world, are updated annually and are available in many major libraries. Or write the Superintendent of Documents (U.S. Printing Office, Washington, DC 20402) for subscription information.

In preparing to sell your work to foreign magazines, you'll also need to become an expert on the foreign marketplace. Although *Writer's Market* lists a few overseas publications, you'll find more extensive information in these sources:

- *Willing's Press Guide* (Thomas Skinner Directories, Windsor Court, East Grinstead House, East Grinstead, West Sussex RH19 1XA, England) lists more than twenty-one thousand publications worldwide and is unrivaled in its coverage of United Kingdom markets.

- Strawberry Media (2460 Lexington Dr., Owosso, Michigan 48867) sells a $15 list of foreign markets seeking English-language material.

TRAVEL ARRANGEMENTS

Even though your article has sold in North America, you must treat it as a fresh idea when pitching it to foreign markets. And that means producing new query letters for the article. (You should send only a clip with a cover letter telling what rights you are offering if the article was originally published in a prestigious, "name" periodical, or if an editor asks for clips.) As always, you'll want to study back issues of target magazines and write your query letters with each magazine's readers in mind.

And you'll want to ask yourself, "What makes me — an American writer — the right person for this assignment?" In your letter, answer the question in a way that will convince foreign editors, who'll be asking the same question.

A common mistake among writers approaching international markets for the first time is sending queries and manuscripts that say *America*. Take, for instance, a query containing the words *color*, *flavor* and *catalog*. If your potential market is in the United Kingdom, these words might better be spelled as the English do: *colour*, *flavour* and *catalogue*.

Picky? Perhaps. In fact, minor spelling differences will not usually block an assignment for an article that otherwise fits the magazine's needs. But for borderline proposals, "proper" spelling can make a difference.

A greater cause for rejection is the use of Americanized language. No matter how common a piece of slang or jargon is in the United States, there's no room for it in a query or article ticketed for overseas. "There is a very American flavour to the writing in your script," read a London literary agent's recent letter to me, "which I take to be your deliberately slangy approach. But this makes it inaccessible to British readers."

As you revise your articles for foreign readers, also be wary of using U.S. statistics and authorities. Authoritative information obtained from people or agencies known to the magazine's audience is often a strong selling point and should be emphasized in your query. For my article on top retirement Edens of the world, I included quotes from Italian businesspeople, German expatriates, Australian government officials, and foreign and American retirees. The piece sold to the Swedish inflight *Scanorama* and to *The Robb Report* in the United States.

Once you receive the green light from a foreign editor, submit a smooth, clean copy of your manuscript — not a clip of the previously published article. Remember, you must treat each article as if it were an original sale.

You'll also want to include with your submission a self-addressed envelope and enough International Reply Coupons (IRCs) to cover return postage. (IRCs are available at your post office. One IRC covers the postage for a one-ounce package at surface-mail rates.) Always use airmail to send your submissions, as surface-mail can take months to arrive. (Once I establish a working relationship with an editor, I cut postage costs by using airgrams — letter-envelope combinations designed for airmail — for queries and correspondence.)

Pay rates and other contract arrangements vary as widely in foreign markets as they do here. Editors may ask writers unknown to them to work on speculation at first; previously published articles may earn less than original work; and payment time may be on acceptance or on publication. As when dealing with North American editors, clarify such matters *before* submitting your manuscript. (I often include an invoice for the agreed-on fee with my manuscript.) When your check arrives, it will likely be payable in the currency of the magazine's home country and not U.S. dollars. In most cases, this won't be a problem as long as you deposit it into your bank account. The bank may charge a fee for handling foreign checks, the check may take longer to clear, and few banks will cash the check on the spot.

RIGHTS OF PASSAGE

One of the nicest aspects of selling articles internationally is that you can approach many markets at once. Unless you query more than one magazine in the same country, you are technically not submitting multiple queries — despite the fact that you might have ten queries out on the same subject at the same time. The key to making the most of your foreign sales is to avoid approaching competing markets and to judiciously parcel out the rights to each article.

Successfully reselling your work in foreign markets depends on retaining as many rights to your work as possible. That begins with your first sale in North America; by selling only first North American serial rights (that is, the right of first magazine publication in North America), you keep the opportunity to sell the work overseas (as well as to market book rights and reprint rights in North America). Pursue a similar policy in international sales, offering first or English-language rights in the magazine's geographic area — such as first English-language rights in Germany or Australian serial rights. When selling to high-paying markets, the added income may justify the publication's request for all rights in a given country — such as all France rights. A similar request often comes from inflight magazines, which seek first rights in their geographic locations, as well as exclusive rights to the inflight market.

Another opportunity for sales is dividing rights by language. Let's say, for example, that you query a Spanish-language magazine in Argentina. If you offer first Spanish-language Argentine rights, you are still free to offer the same piece to an English-language publication in Argentina (and there are English-language magazines nearly everywhere). Be open with editors in all your dealings. But if they object to your retaining individual language rights, their purchase price should be higher.

Translations should always be the periodical's responsibility, and most magazines that deal with foreign-language materials retain translation agencies and at least one editor who reads submissions in English. If you prefer to work with only English-language publications, you might consider sending clips to a foreign syndication agent and asking him to sell foreign-language rights only.

Just how well-traveled your articles become is limited only by the universality of your ideas and your marketing skills. Take those articles lying fallow since their North American sales, and pack them off to editors abroad. Offer first European rights, first Asian rights, first rights to individual countries, exclusive rights to a particular market, reprint rights, and any other rights you can think of — and that are yours to sell. Don't overlook any paying market. If an editor offers $800 for first rights in England, take it. If someone else offers $25 for reprint rights, take that, too. This so-called free money can add up to thousands of dollars a year, more than enough to support your own travels.

How to Chart Your Path to the Bestseller List

Russell Galen

There's a fellow named Lou Aronica who used to run the Spectra science fiction and fantasy imprint at Bantam Books. I knew Lou at the beginning of his career when he was the assistant to another editor to whom I'd sold some westerns, so a few years ago when Lou was promoted into the Spectra job, I made a submission to him immediately. It was a first novel by someone who'd gotten a bit of attention in the magazines.

Lou called me quickly and started firing questions about the author. How old was he? Did he have a job? If so, was it a lifelong career or merely something to keep bread on the table over the short run? What were his next four or five books going to be about? How long did it take for this man to write a completed manuscript? Where did he want to be ten years from now as an author?

I answered all the questions and then said: "Excuse me, Lou. Did you like the manuscript or not?"

"Of course I liked it," he said. "The guy is brilliant — you know that."

"So, are you making an offer for it, or what?"

"I'll make an offer when and if I'm convinced that this is an author for whom we can build a master plan for the future."

And I said to myself, this guy is going to go far. (Lou progressed from being an editor to publishing director of a vastly expanded Spectra program, and a vice-president of Bantam to, most recently, the position of senior vice-president and publisher of the Berkley Publishing Group.) Most editors think only of the book that's being offered: Will it or won't it sell? But the smartest of them are interested in finding authors, not just books. They know that the biggest successes come from long-term master publishing plans that stretch over many books. (Incidentally, Lou liked the author's ideas for future books and was impressed by his plan to quit his job one day and write full time. I wound up selling him the novel plus the author's next three books.)

If you're an author who is not already highly successful, whether you're on your first or your twentieth book, understand something right now: You're a risk — probably a big risk. These days, a book must sell a lot of copies to make even a small profit, and the odds are that unless you have a guaranteed blockbuster, your book is going to lose money.

So why should a publisher even give you the time of day? Because, unless your cover letter begins by saying, "By the time you read this, I will have thrown myself off the Brooklyn Bridge," *you have potential.* Who's to say, no matter how modest your achievements are, that your next book, or your ninth, won't be the book that is so successful that it will put all three of that publisher's kids through college? Just as the bomb squad must view every paper bag as a potential bomb, the publisher must view every author — and I mean *every* — as a potential star.

This point of view has been rising dramatically in the past couple of years, as midlist, modest-selling books drop in sales and the industry becomes more blockbuster-obsessed. This is because blockbusters are hard to find. An editor might get lucky and have Stephen King decide he wants to leave his publisher and come with him; more often, he must grow his own stars, find beginning authors with potential and then groom and develop them. More and more editors now understand that if they want to be successful in the year 2000, they'd better start looking now for the authors who'll be successful in the year 2000, not just the ones who are successful now.

Which brings us to you. Where will you be in the year 2000? If you don't know the answer to that question, you need a master plan — a sense of where you want your writing career to go so you can make decisions based on whether your actions bring you closer to or farther from that goal. A complete guide to forming a master plan for your own career follows, but it should be easy to understand the basic idea: You should start thinking not just in terms of "How do I get this current project sold?" but also "What steps should I be taking now that eventually will get my work on the bestseller list?"

You don't really need to know about all this if you *just* want to get a sale. But you do if you want to be very successful one day, partly because having a master plan is your best bet at being successful, and partly because the editors with long-term visions are the ones who can take you to the top and thus the ones to whom you most want to sell. You won't get them interested unless you learn to speak their language, and learn what they're looking for and how to convince them that you're it.

Before you start building your plan, let's go over the ground rules these editors follow in what I like to call Long-Term Land.

GALEN'S GUIDE TO LONG-TERM LAND

• *The word* inexperienced *isn't the pejorative in this language that it usually is.* Remember that in Long-Term Land, there are only three states of being: on the rise, successful and washed-up. If you're not already successful, it's far better to paint yourself as on the way up than as having had your shot and blown it. Thus, while you might ordinarily be tempted to bloat a résumé and make yourself out to have been around awhile, that will backfire here. The writer with twenty unspectacular book credits looks not like a solid pro, but like someone who has already peaked.

Of course, if you *have* been around awhile, all is far from lost: There are other ways around this problem. Even the most cynical editor realizes that it can take some writers a long time to hit their stride. Authors like Martin Cruz Smith and Marion Zimmer Bradley published scores of paperbacks and were around for decades before finally producing the hardcover bestsellers — *Gorky Park* (Random House) and *The Mists of Avalon* (Ballantine) respectively — that made them famous. Great manuscripts, aggressive agents and imaginative, open-minded publishers made it possible. The point is that Cruz's and Bradley's track records were obstacles to be overcome; you must understand this and be careful of the way you describe your track record.

• *Similarly, it's better to be young.* I'll be blunt and tell you, at the risk of offending or disappointing some readers, that I'm nervous about taking on a new client "of a certain age," unless, of course, he or she is already highly successful. It's hard to tell an editor with a straight face that a sixty-year-old is poised to take off on a brilliant career; again, it does happen, but it's hard to get an editor to believe it. Even if the older writer does become successful, how many years does he have left during which he, I and his publisher can reap the rewards?

Of course, I'll take on and sell a truly good book by an author of any age even if I don't believe a big breakthrough is coming. And there are many editors who are blind to this issue (and most of the others I'll be discussing). But for the best editors, being fifty or older is a negative, though not an insurmountable one. If your book is just so-so, I might take it on if you're a promising newcomer, but not if you're an old-timer. Long-Term Land is like the beach: Being young helps.

• *Understand that these editors are buying you, not just your manuscript.* They want to be convinced that you are dedicated to becoming successful; that you have more than one book in you; that your present work is better than your past work, and that your future work will be even better; that you're looking for a publishing relationship, a long-term home for your work, and not just a deal. Learn which of your qualities are assets in the long term and emphasize them; learn which are negatives and de-emphasize them.

Don't boast that you can write a novel in eleven days, as one writer did to me recently, when an editor is looking for evidence that you take pains to make each book as good as it can possibly be. Don't boast that you always meet your deadlines, when that is far less important to editors than evidence that you strive to make each book better than the one before. Don't mention that you're sure the book you're working on now is going to be a hit, when we really want to hear that you're aiming so high and thinking so grandly that, far from being cocky about your success, you're scared to death you might fail. Don't tell the editor that you're not devoted to, but are merely dabbling in, the genre of your present submission. (What romance editor, for example, looking for writers who can be built into stars, is going to respond to a letter from a mystery writer saying, "I thought I'd give this genre a whirl, just to get a break from my regular stuff"?)

• *Don't be afraid to reveal that inside you is a seething, fiery core of ambition and lust for success that would appall Napoleon.*

DRAWING UP YOUR BATTLE PLAN

Michael McQuay isn't out to rule France, but he is an ambitious writer. After writing and selling — without an agent — his first five science fiction novels, Mike sensed that something was wrong with his career. He knew he was good, but his sales didn't really show it. There was no growth, no sense that things would improve if he'd just hang in and keep writing.

So he came to me and we hammered out a master plan. That was several years ago, and while his story is still far from its ending, it is far enough along to illustrate some basic points about your own master plan.

• *It isn't any easier or quicker to become a successful writer than it is to become a brain surgeon.* Kids in their first year of medical school don't whine to their professors, "When do we start making some real money, sir?" They know they have ten years of schooling ahead of them first. Writing a successful book isn't any easier than slicing away at people's cerebrums, and it takes just as long to learn how to do it right.

I'll give you the same warning I gave Mike: It will be five years before you see any results from the plan at all and ten years before you achieve your goal.

• *Andrew Carnegie's advice for becoming wealthy is important: "Put all your eggs into one basket and then watch that basket."* I studied McQuay's writing and determined that his strength was in his savagely powerful characters and strong story lines. Therefore, mainstream suspense fiction, which showcases these same elements, was going to be the field in which he would one day make his stand. From that moment on, every choice we made, every new story he created, was designed to further his reputation in this one field. He still wrote science fiction at that point because that's where the easy sales came for him, but his science fiction became increasingly realistic, less farfetched and exotic. He gradually would move over to writing exclusively mainstream suspense fiction.

There's not much overlap between groups of readers. Romance readers don't read westerns; thriller readers don't buy biographies; and so on. So if you're bouncing around doing many different kinds of books, you're reaching different audiences with each book. Individual readers aren't staying with you from book to book, forming a loyalty to you; they're reading only the one book you've written for them and then abandoning you. By contrast, if you stay in the same field, readers in that field will be reading two, three, four books by you in a row, and becoming loyal fans.

By building on this core audience, you can create momentum. With each new book, you only have to find a small group of new readers in order to have sales figures that are going steadily up. Let's say that a new book can, with luck, find 100,000 readers who had never before heard of the author. If each new book is in a new field, it must find 100,000 brand new readers every time — and if you slip up even once and sell only 55,000 (which will happen sooner or later), you're seen as someone whose sales are going down — a loser, a has-been. But if you stay in the same field, your second book is going to be picked up pretty much automatically by the 100,000 readers of your first, if it's any good. Thus, you must find only, say, 50,000 brand-new converts in order to have a dramatic increase in your sales. If your new audience base of 150,000 gets you 80,000 new converts for the novel after that, and so on, it's not going to be long before you're selling in the millions.

Decide in advance what kind of writer you want to be, and then bend every effort toward making it in that one field. It's no disaster if you need a little variety now and then and want to do a different kind of book, but you should have a home base.

• *You can't execute a master plan alone.* It's essential that your agent and publisher think in terms of your long-term future and share your hopes and dreams. If your editor feels he has no future with the company, or if your agent is planning to quit as soon as she finds a husband, or if your agent or editor simply can't think beyond tomorrow, you're with the wrong person. Such people — and they are the most common type, so keep an eye out for them — will discourage you from doing what's best for you if it makes this week easier for them.

• *Now is not the time to take it easy.* I want to stress here that a master plan involves far more than cranking out books that hew to some secret formula. More important than all my little points is that you do the work of your life. Mike did. Each book was better than the one before. If the plan had an editorial effect on Mike's work, it was in the tremendous level of inspiration that it supplied him. He felt as if he were working not just to fulfill a contract and get the latest advance, but to achieve something of vast scope, to make a ten-year plan a reality.

It's like the difference between having sex just to have sex and having it because you're trying to make a baby. As all parents will attest, there's something unforgettably intense about the latter, a sense that all your energy is going to create something significant. The first book Mike delivered after we began to work together, *Memories* (Bantam), was a hundred million billion times better than anything he'd written before; it won some important awards and got a lot of attention. The critics started writing reviews like "Who is this guy?" and "From a completely unexpected source comes one of the best novels of the year." Part of the phenomenon was McQuay's own discovery of just how good he really was, but part of it, I like to think, came from my whispering "Plan . . . plan . . . plan" into his ear all the time, reminding him that he was working for something Jupiter-sized and that there was someone in New York who believed he could do it.

The great goal of your plan should bring great work out of you. Every book must be your absolute best to take you closer to achieving your goal, or it will have the effect of taking you backward. If you're in the mood to try something goofy, something light, something uncommercial, something dangerous, it would be better to save that for after you've achieved your goals.

What all of this is really about is *building your audience*. Newer writers are cursed by one terrible plague: small readerships, rarely more than six thousand in hardcover, fifty thousand in paperback. Those audiences are too small to make anything happen, to generate the kind of word of mouth you need for a book to become a bestseller. As in atomic physics, these audiences are too small to start a chain reaction — they're beneath critical mass. So you must build your audience, get it to the point where it's big enough to generate word of mouth that will get you an even bigger audience that will generate even bigger word of mouth, and so on. Avoid anything that decreases your audience even for one book, causes it merely to remain steady for one book, or causes it to have only a small rise for one book.

McQuay and I decided that he should stay with his current publisher. As luck would have it, his five previous books had been acquired by Bantam, and his editor was Lou Aronica (who acquired both science fiction and mainstream fiction). Since we already had precisely the kind of editor we wanted — one who would accept short-term problems and sacrifices if they served a long-term goal — there was no need to think in terms of finding a new home for him.

• *Momentum is everything*. The next part of the plan involved McQuay's delivering a new book roughly every nine months. Fortunately, with Aronica and Bantam willing participants in the plan, I anticipated no difficulty in getting sales every nine months. In fact, the first deal I negotiated under the plan was for two books, so that McQuay could begin the second immediately after delivering the first, rather than having to wait for new negotiations, new contracts, etc. After that, we did a four-book deal.

Audiences have short memories. They can enjoy a book, buy it in huge numbers, and then, eighteen months later, not even remember the author's name. Nine to twelve months is about the right interval between books; the new book catches an audience that has fond memories of the previous one. This is a very big problem for writers who also hold down full-time jobs, but I'm afraid that if your job prevents you from doing more than one book every two years, there's a much smaller chance you'll ever make enough from your writing to be able to quit that job.

These figures are for paperback originals. It's different with hardcover, because a paperback reprint will appear one year after the hardcover and keep readers' memories of your work alive. I advise most of my hardcover clients to have no more than one new book out every other year.

This involves making each book your very best, with no lapses or detours. And it involves bending every issue to the question of whether it contributes to building your audience. A decision that in any way compromises the goal of building the audience is a mistake, even if it involves a short-term benefit (such as taking a higher advance from a weak publisher that is overpaying in order to build up its list but that can't distribute its books effectively).

You may also need to make short-term sacrifices in order to further your long-term goals. For example, you might be running low on money when along comes a publisher who needs you to do a quick novel in the Young Nurses in Love series, and he won't let you use a pseudonym. Refuse: Having your name on such a book might make it harder for another publisher to take you seriously. Or you might want to postpone that uncommercial labor of love until later in your career when you can better afford to have your sales figures take a sudden drop. Or you might want to spend some time on a magazine article that won't make you much money but that will get your work in front of a new audience, an audience that might then start buying your books. Make your business decisions based on how they affect your master plan.

• *When you've done all the planning you can do and laid all the groundwork you can lay, the time has come to go for the Big One.* Mike McQuay and I bided our time. Then he came to me one day with an idea for a book that I thought would be a blockbuster. This is the key moment in the master plan: What you have been preparing for all these years is the marketing, selling, writing and publishing of a Big Book.

The problem was that Mike's idea was so much more ambitious and daring than anything he'd ever written that he was afraid no publisher, even his own, would believe he could bring it off. But I knew he was ready and advised him to write the entire manuscript on spec (that is, without a contract); we would then offer publishers the proven, finished commodity. This involved a spectacular sacrifice for Mike; while working without a contract, his income dried up because he couldn't work simultaneously on his bread-and-butter science fiction projects. Our agency loaned him some money, he took some breaks now and then to work on write-for-hire projects, and he managed, over a year, to write about 250 pages of the novel plus a one-hundred-page proposal.

This seemed to be sufficient for our purposes, and I showed the material to Lou Aronica with a little speech about how our years of working together to bring Mike McQuay along had finally borne fruit. I told him we were going to want $100,000 for it—ten times what McQuay had ever received before. While Aronica didn't say anything, there was that little sound in the throat editors sometimes make that I translate as, "You %*$*%#%$ agent! Are you out of your *@%$@%* mind?" What a nice sound it is.

Well, Aronica took the material home and read it. He called me, and you know what he said? He said, "You want $100,000 for this book?"

And I, getting ready for a fight, said, "That's right, and not a penny less."

And he said, "Could I have two for that price?"

And that's how Michael McQuay, some fifteen years after becoming a professional writer, became an overnight success with a $200,000 deal.

For the next step in the plan, we go for seven figures.

(Let me be fully accurate here and say for the record that the deal is a complex one in which certain conditions must be fulfilled for the entire $200,000 to be paid. However, the deal still guarantees McQuay a minimum of $150,000.)

IT'S NEVER TOO SOON

I realize that many of you would be happy just to get a sale and may be thinking that it'll be years before you need to worry about any of this stuff, if ever. But even if you're still dreaming about sales, it's not too soon for you to put a plan like this into effect.

There are three reasons.

• Editors look for writers who think this way. Thus, when your chance at that first sale comes, you could easily blow it by answering the editor's questions in the wrong way. If the editor asks "Can you do new books at the rate of one a year?" you must know that the right answer is *Yes*.

• Even at the beginning of your career, you're making decisions about what to write, about where to concentrate your resources. You need to make these decisions with your long-term goals in mind, because mistakes made at the beginning of a career can take years to undo. If you decide that investigative journalism, for example, is the basket into which you want to put all your eggs, it's important for you to realize that it's a mistake to begin your career with a romance novel just because you have a shot at an easy sale. You'll be typecast as a romance writer, and editors of investigative journalism books may never take you seriously.

• As I'm sure you've already learned, nothing in the world is more discouraging than the early years of a writing career. Having a master plan reminds you that, tough as those first steps might be, they are steps nevertheless, the beginnings of a journey toward a specific destination. The sense that you're working toward something, no matter how distant it may sometimes seem, is a hell of a lot more inspiring and exciting than the sense that you're flailing around, collecting random rejection slips. It keeps your eyes on the prize, as the saying goes.

When to Quit Your Day Job

Dana K. Cassell

Just about every writer who's sold an article or a story has daydreamed about writing full time. A lot of us have even chucked our day jobs and tried to make a go of it. Unfortunately, many part-timers find themselves unable to make the transition to self-supporting, full-time writing.

Sometimes they fail because of lack of preparation; more frequently they simply fail to follow their plans.

My own personal experiences — which reflect those of a couple thousand other writers I've met while serving as executive director of a freelance writers' network — convinced me that a successful full-time freelance writing career demands both ability *and* attention to a variety of critical technical concerns.

ABILITY

You wouldn't undertake a cross-country auto trip without first knowing how to drive and having an able vehicle. Likewise, before going full-time, it makes sense to have some assurances that you're a sufficiently capable freelance writer.

Note that I used the adjectives *capable freelance* writer and not *great* writer. Successful, money-making, full-time freelancers are not necessarily the best writers around. They *do* have the ability to target readers with appropriate material and to communicate effectively with those readers.

Unfortunately, there's no "writer's license" test to tell you when your skills are equal to the challenge of the full-time route. But there are criteria you can use to test youself.

Some hopeful full-timers hone and evaluate their writing skills through staff jobs with newspapers, magazines or corporations before freelancing seriously. If you can satisfy your readers and superiors in

166

a writing-related job for a few years, you should feel secure in your ability to communicate well on paper.

Many of us simply learn by doing. I remember my own early free-lance days, when I was "becoming a writer." Whatever *Writer's Digest* said to do that month is what I wrote — until the next issue came out and I tried *its* suggestions. The sales were sporadic at first, as I learned, tested my skills in the marketplace and refined my material. Then, after five years with a total of twenty-one freelance sales, I suddenly sold twenty-eight manuscripts during a single year. The following year, I maintained the pace, with thirty-two additional sales. It was during that year I felt secure enough about my ability to consider writing full time.

Writer Christine Adamec (*The Encyclopedia of Adoption*) decided to make her move after she started selling magazine features on a regular basis. "When I always had an assignment to work on, so there wasn't any down time, I realized I could actually use the word *writer* to describe myself. Once I'd overcome that hesitation to think of myself as a writer, I was able to go full time. At that time I was selling at least two or three magazine features a month."

As critical as it is to communicate effectively with readers, you also must be able to target those readers with appropriate material. Rare is the writer who is kept busy solely from assignments initiated by editors. Sure, once editors learn you are available full time and thus more likely to be able to meet short or emergency deadlines, you can expect a few more phone calls. Consider those assignments the gravy — they're a bonus for your writing business, not the basis for it.

Your day-to-day, routine meat-and-potatoes work will result from the query letters and proposals you send to editors. Therefore, you must feel secure in your ability to submit the right ideas to the right publications at the right time — most of the time. No writer scores with *every* idea the first time. But you at least need to be able to make a hit often enough to produce adequate income to stay in business.

And that rule is absolute regardless of the field you write in.

Measuring your ability according to these factors only tells you if you're equipped to meet the challenge of full-time freelancing. Whether or not you can make the transition successfully will depend on how well you follow your plan — allowing sufficient time for such technical concerns as marketing, administration, production and study. These "part-time" tasks will make or break you as a full-time writer, so let's discuss each one in detail.

MARKETING

Marketing can be defined as selecting, selling, advertising, packaging and delivering goods or services. It is critical to your success. Without it, even the most eloquent writing will sit in a desk drawer unread.

When I discovered this basic truth, I went from being a writing hobbyist to a full-time writer. As I've already described, my part-time efforts were varied; sales ranged from children's short stories to greeting card verse to women's nonfiction to business articles.

When I decided to get serious about my writing, I started with the selection phase of marketing and analyzed my sales up to that point. I listed each sale according to type of material (puzzle, juvenile fiction, trade journal article, women's article, etc.). Then I compared the number of ideas queried in each field with the number of go-aheads or assignments in each field. Next I compared the number of manuscripts submitted in each field with the number of sales in each field. By comparing ratios, I found that apparently my natural market was the trade journal field; it was there that I needed the fewest number of queries mailed to generate the most go-aheads received, and where I earned the highest manuscript-submission-to-manuscript-sale ratio. Therefore, I concentrated on the trade journal field when I went full time.

You may not *want* to specialize in a single subject or market area, but at least give the idea serious thought. Virtually every full-time writer I've known concentrates in one or two areas. Jackie Denalli, a full-time business magazine freelancer, said that if she were to begin her writing career over again, she would be "more focused. For a while I couldn't decide what I wanted to do, and I'd flitter from one thing to another. Once I made up my mind that I couldn't write absolutely fabulous short fiction, and really good business articles, and the Great American Novel, *and* a how-to book all at the same time, I became more productive and my income went up."

When you focus (or concentrate or specialize) your writing in one, two or even three areas, several benefits result:

• You have a better chance of reusing your costly (in terms of time and money) research. A hobbyist can afford to spend sixteen hours and several dollars researching a piece just because it's interesting, but the successful full-time professional uses that research to write and sell additional related articles — raising her overall dollar-per-hour-invested rate. I like to call this "making your research earn its keep."

• Editors soon perceive you as an "expert," and give you more assignments. One editor assigns me at least an article every year on a security topic. Although I sent her several queries over a period of many months on that subject years ago, I never did score with one of my ideas. But — and this is why specialization can pay off — she called *me* when she later wanted one of her ideas on a related subject written. My concentration in several business subjects (security, marketing, retailing) has also led to assigned article series — even one seven-article supplement.

• Because you soon build comprehensive reference/source files in a specialty field, future writing in that field will be easier and faster — and, therefore, more profitable. For example, I'd already written and sold more than a hundred articles on retail advertising/promotion when I proposed my book, *How to Advertise and Promote Your Retail Store.* Not only did this experience help me get the book contract, it made writing the book a breeze.

You don't need to resign yourself to writing about *only* one subject for the rest of your career. That's boring. Writing about something different, or trying a new writing field once in a while, keeps life interesting, forestalls writer's block and can even lead to unexpected profit centers.

The success secret is to concentrate at least 80 percent of your efforts in your proven field(s), then experiment with, or test new fields with, up to 20 percent. Periodically reexamine your ratios, and you'll note declining subjects and markets *before* they become cold, as well as spot new ones to pursue while they're still hot.

I've already mentioned the importance of making the most of one's research and material by slanting, reslanting, reworking and reprinting. Duane Newcomb's book *A Complete Guide to Marketing Magazine Articles* taught me this lesson and helped me begin to make real money writing. It's now out of print, although much of it has been included in his *How to Sell and Re-Sell Your Writing* (Writer's Digest Books).

When you get into reslanting and reselling, you soon realize that your income-per-hour is more important than your income-per-sale. This is another concept that separates most part-timers from full-timers. It's easy, when writing is an avocation, to look solely at how much money an article will bring from a particular magazine before submitting it.

But the successful full-timer looks further than the numbers on the check. When you have only a limited number of hours a week to meet your income needs, the number of work hours it will take to earn a particular fee becomes as important as the amount. A $100 payment for a reprint that takes fifteen minutes to submit pays a better hourly wage than does a new $800 article that takes twenty hours to research and write (with related research costs). For this reason, the full-timer considers *total* income potential before tackling any project.

I've spent a chunk of space here on marketing because it's so important. I used to tell workshop audiences that effective marketing was 90 percent of writing success, but no one wanted to believe it, so I dropped back to 80 percent. (But it's really closer to 90 percent for most full-time writers.)

ADMINISTRATION

Attention to the administration side of business also takes on added importance when you become a full-time freelancer—a fact that dismays many "creative" types. It's unusual, in fact, to find a writer who welcomes record-keeping and other administrative chores. Full-time magazine writer David Kohn says, "A business really consists of two parts: One is doing well what you do; the other is running a business that does well doing what you do. I think I write well, but I'm still learning a lot about running a business, and I don't know that I'm a natural entrepreneurial type. It's always difficult to be a businessperson if you're not naturally inclined that way. Unfortunately, it's also a necessity."

Certainly, maintaining records to keep the IRS happy is necessary and important for all income-producing writers. But the full-time writer is a small-business owner and must manage the business in addition to selling and writing.

Among the administrative or management areas of concern are planning, time management, purchasing, maintenance and financial management.

Each management area could fill an article of its own; in fact, several general small-business management books are available on each of these topics. It's a good idea to keep a few current ones near your desk for study and reference, but we can touch on some of these topics now.

Planning covers everything from tomorrow's schedule to annual marketing plans. Once you've worked out goals and a sales strategy, you know how many queries, proposals, brochures or whatever to send each week or each day. You also will need a production plan: How many articles, stories, outlines, scripts, etc., are you going to work on or complete each week or each month?

Writers who have been squeezing in writing hours among regular jobs, household chores and family obligations often enter full-time life figuring they'll now have all the time in the world. *Beware this trap!*

Too much time often leads to procrastination and *less* productivity than a busy part-timer might achieve. So time use is an important management area. The full-time writer usually has more control over working hours and can consider the body's circadian rhythms when scheduling different kinds of work.

Management of those work hours becomes especially critical when assignments pile up and that scheduled forty-hour week stretches into fifty—even sixty or more—hours. Thus, you need to employ these basic time-management principles:

- Consolidate similar tasks (correspondence, phone calls, filing, errands).
- Tackle tough, important jobs first.
- Delegate to family members, job-hungry high school students and independent contractors certain tasks (such as stuffing/labeling, breaking down long-distance phone records, typing/word processing, interview-tape transcriptions, household chores).
- Decide which paperwork can be streamlined or eliminated.
- Log and analyze time use.
- Establish priorities.
- Maintain energy with exercise breaks, appropriate foods, proper lighting.
- Streamline mail handling and telephone techniques.

When writing income is used to pay for life's necessities, and not primarily the extras (as part-time writing income frequently is), the administration of that income achieves new prominence. Purchases of equipment, supplies and maintenance contracts take additional planning and study. The chore of managing an unpredictable income can make or break the full-timer fast.

PRODUCTION

This is our actual business: producing articles, stories, books, ad copy, video scripts and so on. Therefore, a significant portion of our time must necessarily be spent on production. (I'll pass on my recommendations shortly.)

If you frequently run up against writer's block or consistently miss deadlines as a part-time writer, those syndromes will not disappear when you go full time. If anything, they will get worse when the stress of unpaid bills or the crunch of several assignments mounts.

To be successful, the full-time writer must juggle the research of six or eight different projects, the writing of five or six drafts in varying stages of completion, possibly two or three photographic sessions, plus the polishing and submission of three or four additional projects — all in the same week. It helps to be organized; the disorganized "creative" type sometimes runs into problems.

While I stressed earlier the importance of becoming known in a few subject or skill areas, most writers I've watched succeed as full-timers have kept their options open. Wise use of that 20 percent experimental writing I suggested can make a big difference.

Because I talked to so many business owners and managers while researching business articles, plus specialized in articles on advertising/promotion, it wasn't long before I was approached to write ad copy, brochure copy and public relations material.

Although I've never pushed to make this a major portion of my writing business (I prefer to write articles and books), it has provided quick money when needed, has led me to new business sources, and has stimulated new article or book chapter ideas. Plus, I appreciate some variety.

Joseph Straub knows firsthand the value of reserving some production time for different kinds of work or clients. "For over a year, I edited a management newsletter, which was wonderful work. The pay was great, but with one phone call, management canceled the newsletter through no fault of mine, and bam, I was out of a job. That one experience taught me to never, ever rely on one client or one field. I like to keep my options open."

From these examples, you can see how, to the successful full-time writer, production means more than meeting a few deadlines. It includes scheduling the different components of production to maximize time use, plus deciding *what* to produce so as to keep current clients and editors happy, as well as preparing for future business needs.

Most of all, it requires assuming the posture of a "communicator with words" rather than that of solely an article writer (or whatever).

STUDY

The most successful full-time freelancers I know are the first to attend seminars and conferences, read books on writing, and generally keep learning. Study *is* a very important tool.

There are always bad writing habits to spot and break, and good ones to pick up; new fields to explore and consider; and other writers to share experiences with and learn from. The more established a writer becomes, the less he or she usually learns from seminar speakers, but the more benefits spending a day with other writers can offer: from "brain-picking" about methods, markets and contracts to simply finding rejuvenation outside our solitary offices.

Over the years, I've accumulated an extensive library of books and tapes targeted to writers. Their main value to me has been as motivating tools: Reading a couple chapters a day, or one book a week, or listening to a tape while exercising or washing dishes does more to energize my creativity than educate my brain. And for the full-time writer, *that* can be more important. Some writers judiciously schedule writing seminars for this very reason; whenever their spirits begin to sag or the office walls begin to close in, they will use a seminar as a B-12 shot.

Likewise, virtually all full-time writers I know read several writers' magazines and newsletters — always keeping on top of the latest market information, publishing trends, new areas to pursue, and so on.

SCHEDULING

How in the world does a person cover all these areas? With scheduling.

Every situation is different, but a basic starting place for planning is to allocate your time and energy in the following proportions:

Marketing — 25 percent
Administration — 12½ percent
Production — 50 percent
Study — 12½ percent

This is only a starting point, a rule of thumb. If your full-time business will consist of two or three novels a year, you may decide to reduce the marketing and administration percentages while increasing the production — and maybe emphasizing the study a bit more. Or, if your business is largely high-fee, direct-mail copy, you may need to allocate more time to marketing and less to production.

OK, so now you've completed your preparation, and you know you're ready to make the jump to a full-time career. Will you succeed?

I've watched enough people go from beginners or part-timers to successful full-timers over the past nine years to offer an enthusiastic "Yes, you can. . . ."

But, during the same time, I've also watched a good number try it and not make it. So I temper my enthusiasm with ". . . but it isn't always easy."

You need to take a long, hard, honest look at yourself and your situation. Will you carefully lay out and closely follow your plan? Do you have the ability to communicate effectively with readers and to target those readers with appropriate material? And do you have the financial cushion to carry you through the dry spells?

Yes?

Congratulations.

v.
The Final Reward

Psychic Income

Gary Turbak

I don't write for the joy of it. I write to get paid. But sometimes I get paid in joy.

Most writers already know that the road to riches doesn't run through their backyards. In fact, a writer's remuneration can be down-right disappointing; but this is the case only if that writer neglects to count his psychic income in the tally.

Psychic income is the benefit of writing that we store in our minds, not our bank accounts. You can't use your psychic income to buy groceries and gasoline, but it's valuable nonetheless.

In 1982, I was paid one of the biggest psychic income bonuses I ever hope to receive. While writing an article about missing children for *Kiwanis* magazine, I found myself becoming personally involved in this horrific tragedy. Each year, upwards of ten thousand kids vanish from backyards and playgrounds, and no one does much about it. Police often can't locate a missing child, forcing heartbroken parents to conduct their own inadequate searches.

One Florida mother, Katheleen Mancil, had a particularly poignant tale to tell, and — via lengthy phone conversations — I got to know Katheleen quite well. Her daughter Marian, in her midteens, had been missing for two years, and Katheleen and her husband (the girl's step-father) had been searching futilely all that time. They repeatedly re-ceived reports that Marian had been seen in this truck stop or that café, but it was never the right girl. A desperate, all-night race into Georgia turned up an incredible teenage look-alike — but no daughter. More than once, crank callers said they had seen the girl being raped or beaten. Katheleen developed cancer, and the money ran out, but she never gave up hope.

"Please help me find my baby," Katheleen pleaded during our conversations. "I just need to know that she's all right." I told her that maybe my article would help, but I didn't really believe it would bring her daughter home. I eventually used Katheleen's story as my lead:

About 8:30 A.M. on Jan. 7, 1980, Katheleen Mancil drove her daughter, Marian Batson, to school in Inverness, Florida. "See you tonight," Katheleen called as the petite, blue-eyed sixteen-year-old stepped from the car.

But she did not see Marian that night. Or the next. Or the next.

No one remembers seeing Marian after she left her mother's car. The day after her disappearance, her purse was found in a trash can about twenty-five miles from the school. She had joined the swelling ranks of children simply labeled "MISSING."

The story was published in *Kiwanis* magazine. When *Reader's Digest* reprinted the article, the editors requested photos of missing children to run with the story, and I put them in touch with Katheleen.

Soon after the magazine hit the streets, my phone rang early one morning. It was Katheleen. "Gary, I've got my baby back!" she said. A reader in Georgia had seen Marian's picture, and the teen was now safely back home. My friend Katheleen wept as she told me the details of their loving reunion. Two thousand miles away, I was fighting back the tears of joy, too — and bursting with pride. *That* is psychic income, and few people have as great an earning potential as do writers.

Psychic installments from my involvement in the missing-child tragedy continued to come my way for several months. *Reader's Digest* asked me to write a follow-up story about Marian Batson, flying me to Florida to interview her, Katheleen and the people who had found the girl. This second article carried more photos of missing kids. At last count, twenty-three missing children have been located as a result of the photos accompanying my two stories, and I've had the pleasure of talking with several extremely grateful parents.

But not all psychic salary arrives in such a dramatic pay envelope. On occasion, my account bulges with more subtle deposits. An article I wrote about game poaching for *Field & Stream* has made sportsmen more aware of this serious problem. "I knew poaching was bad, but I had no idea it was as bad as 'The New Poachers' [the title of my article] shows it to be," said one reader in a letter to the editor. "I hope you will continue to print articles to turn people off making a profit at our wildlife's expense," wrote another.

Public recognition is another automatic deposit in a writer's psychic account. Shortly after my missing-children stories were published, a writer from my local newspaper devoted his weekly column to me, and a radio station in New York called for an interview. You can bet I hurried to the bank with those psychic deposits. And who among writers will ever forget the high that accompanied their first byline? I remember rushing immediately to my wife's place of work when my first contributor copy (of *The American Legion Magazine*) arrived.

Little psychic sums may come your way at a party when a new acquaintance recognizes your name, or when an old friend says he liked your latest story. I have received flattering invitations to address university journalism classes and a gathering of English teachers. Several magazine readers have written or called long distance to tell me they enjoyed my articles. Once, an elderly man in Connecticut read a story of mine about ancient medical practices and insisted on sending me two quaint old medical books. I put all these in my mental piggy bank, too.

Psychic riches may even spill over to members of a writer's family. One day in the checkout line at a supermarket, my wife couldn't resist telling the clerk that I had written the story about missing kids displayed prominently on the overleaf of the nearby copies of *Reader's Digest*. Before my wife left the store, the clerk purchased a copy of the magazine and graciously asked *my wife* to autograph it.

Sometimes, such as with the *Reader's Digest* stories, I am well paid (in dollars) for my work. But long after that money has been spent, I'll still be collecting interest on my psychic income. On dark days when my mailbox bulges with rejection slips, I can lift my spirits to the sky by recalling how my work as a writer has helped reunite families and bring joy to people I will never even meet.

CONTRIBUTORS

Ludmilla Alexander

Ludmilla Alexander is a freelance writer, based in Saratoga, California. Specializing in travel and general interest articles, she is senior editor of *South Bay Accent Magazine*, a lifestyle publication in San José, California. A member of the Society of American Travel Writers, she has also written for *Friendly Exchange*, *National Motorist* and *Relax Magazine*.

Christopher P. Baker

Christopher P. Baker is the author of the *Costa Rica Handbook*, *Travel Bug Guide to California* and *Passport Illustrated Guide to Jamaica*. His articles have appeared in *Newsweek*, *Caribbean Travel and Life*, *Delta Sky*, *USAir Magazine*, *National Wildlife*, *Los Angeles Times*, *Christian Science Monitor* and more than one hundred other publications worldwide.

Michael A. Banks

Michael Banks is the author of forty-eight novels and nonfiction books, including several hobby-oriented titles. A full-time freelance writer since 1983, Banks has also published more than three thousand articles and short stories.

Lawrence Block

Lawrence Block wrote *Writer's Digest*'s fiction column for fourteen years. He has won all the major crime-fiction awards. His most recent novels are *The Devil Knows You're Dead* and *The Burglar Who Traded Ted Williams*.

Louise Boggess

Louise Boggess earned her B.A., M.A. and Phi Beta Kappa from the University of Texas. When her husband's work moved them to San Francisco, she taught professional writing at San Mateo College by classroom, television and videocassette. She teaches correspondence writing courses for the University of California/Berkeley and for Writer's Digest School. She has become nationally known for her three books on how to write and three on American cut glass, co-authored with her husband, Bill. Published in numerous magazines, she has been a staff member on sixty-seven writers conferences.

R. Jean Bryant

R. Jean Bryant, an independent consultant, teacher and writer for more than twenty-five years, is the author of *Anybody Can Write — A Playful Approach: Ideas for the Writer, Beginner and Would-Be Writer*, as well as *Stop Improving Yourself and Start Living* and *Loving Work*.

Dana K. Cassell

Dana K. Cassell is founder and director of Florida Freelance Writers Association, editor of the newsletter *Freelance Writer's Report*, and a writer specializing in business articles and advertising promotion. Author of four books, her most recent,

Encyclopedia of Obesity and Eating Disorders (Facts on File) was published in January 1994.

Marshall J. Cook

Marshall J. Cook is the author of *Freeing Your Creativity: A Writer's Guide* (Writer's Digest Books, 1992) and editor of *Creativity Connection*. He is currently a professor at the University of Wisconsin outreach.

James Dulley

James Dulley began writing the weekly Q&A column "Cut Your Utility Bills" fourteen years ago. His column appears in hundreds of newspapers from California to Maine. His formal education includes a B.S. in engineering, an M.B.A. in marketing and doctoral study in the management of technology at the Harvard Business School.

John D. Engle, Jr.

John Engle's poetry and prose have appeared in hundreds of periodicals from *Commonweal* to *Writer's Digest*. His latest of eight books is entitled *Tree People*. He has received many awards, most recently the Byline Literary Award, the Alabama Award and the Phoenix Writer's Award. He currently teaches writing workshops, self-syndicates a column and is an editorial associate for *Writer's Digest*.

Russell Galen

Russell Galen has been a literary agent since 1976 and is president of Scovil Chichak Galen Literary Agency in New York. "New York Overheard," his column on trends in the publishing industry, appears in *Writer's Digest*.

Judson Jerome

The late Judson Jerome was the *Writer's Digest* poetry columnist for more than thirty years and was the author and editor of numerous books.

Mansfield Latimer

Mansfield Latimer is a retired business consultant who now devotes his time to writing, travel and playing in senior tennis tournaments throughout the country. His writing credits include numerous magazine articles, fiction, poetry and five books, most recently *Never Too Old to Play Tennis: And Never Too Old to Start*, (Betterway Books, 1993). Formerly a newspaper columnist and professional public speaker, he has over fifty years of experience as a seminar leader.

Deanie Francis Mills

Deanie Francis Mills has had four books of suspense published under the name D.F. Mills. Her most recent novel, *Losers, Weepers*, was published in September 1994 under the name Deanie Francis Mills. She has also been published in *Writer's Digest*, *Redbook*, *Good Housekeeping* and *Woman's World*.

James Morgan

James Morgan is the former articles editor of *Playboy* and editorial director of *Southern Magazine*. He has written for *Esquire*, *Gentlemen's Quarterly*, *The Atlantic Monthly*, *The Washington Post Magazine* and others. He is currently working on a book about

Virginia Kelley, President Clinton's mother, to be published in fall 1994 by Simon & Schuster.

Gary Provost

Gary Provost is the author of *High Stakes: Inside the New Las Vegas* and is coproducer and instructor of the Video Novel Workshop.

Maxine Rock

A journalist and author for twenty years, Maxine Rock has written five books and one thousand magazine articles, and has won seventeen journalism awards. In 1993, she was distinguished as "Best Feature Writer" in Georgia and also won the Outstanding Article Award from the American Society of Journalists and Authors.

Candy Schulman

Candy Schulman's articles and essays have appeared in *The New York Times*, *New York Magazine*, *Travel & Leisure*, *Family Circle*, *Writer's Digest* and other publications. She teaches writing at the New School for Social Research in New York City.

Bob Schultz

Bob Schultz has written over one hundred articles for a variety of newspapers and magazines, including *Writer's Digest*, *Capper's*, *Learning*, *People in Action*, *Instructor Magazine* and *Poet's Review*. He has also written fifty book reviews for newspapers in California and for national magazines. He is past editor of the *California State Math Journal*.

Michael H. Sedge

Michael H. Sedge is president of Strawberry Media, Inc., with offices in the United States and Europe. His works appear in publications around the world, such as Singapore Airlines' *Silver Kris* and Italy's *Going Places Doing Things*.

Paul M. Thompson

Paul M. Thompson has been a professional writer for twenty-five years, the last ten in the corporate arena. He is currently a senior writer for a large Detroit-area communications agency and works primarily in the auto industry. He has extensive experience in business writing, including videos, speeches, brochures, direct marketing and training material.

Gary Turbak

Gary Turbak is a full-time freelance writer and the author of six nonfiction books. His most recent book, published in 1993, is entitled *Survivors in the Shadows — Threatened and Endangered Mammals of the American West*, (Northland Press, 1993).

Molly Wigand

Molly Wigand is a former writer-editor for Hallmark Cards. She has been a regular contributor to *Snoopy* and *Mickey Mouse* magazines and is the author of four children's books. She is currently a freelance contributor of social-expression companies and other clients.

INDEX

More Great Books
to Help You Get Published!

Writer's Digest Guide to Good Writing — Put the best advice and inspiration from the past 75 years of *Writer's Digest* magazine to work for you! You'll be inspired by authors like Vonnegut, Sinclair, Michener, Steinbeck, and over a dozen others! *#10391/352 pages/$18.95*

The Writer's Digest Guide to Manuscript Formats — Don't take chances with your hard work! Learn how to prepare and submit books, poems, scripts, stories and more with a professional look editors expect from a good writer. *#10025/198 pages/$18.95*

Beginning Writer's Answer Book — Discover everything you need to know to get published — from how to generate great ideas, to the most up-to-date business advice and tax tips. *#10394/336 pages/$16.95*

Writing the Blockbuster Novel — You'll create the memorable characters, exotic settings, clashing conflicts, and universal plots sure to make your novel a success. *#10393/224 pages/$17.95*

Magazine Writing That Sells — Discover the secrets to sensational queries, in-depth interviewing, reader-grabbing leads, solidly written pieces, and can't miss marketing strategies. *#10409/240 pages/$16.95*

Creating Characters — Learn how to build characters that jump off the page. In-depth instruction shows you how to infuse characters with emotion so powerful they will touch every reader. *#10417/192 pages/$14.99, paperback*

20 Master Plots — Write great contemporary fiction from timeless plots. This guide outlines 20 plots from various genres and illustrates how to adapt them into your own fiction. *#10366/240 pages/$16.95*

Thesaurus of Alternatives to Worn Out Words and Phrases — Rid your work of trite cliches and hollow phrases for good! You'll learn how to vivify your work with alternative, lively and original words! *#10408/$17.99/304 pages/available 9-5-94*

Writing the Short Story — With Bickham's unique "workshop on paper" you'll plan, organize, write, revise, and polish a short story. Clear instruction, helpful charts and practical exercises will lead you every step of the way! *#10421/$16.99/224 pages/available 9-16-94*

Make Your Words Work — Loaded with samples and laced with exercises this guide will help you clean up your prose, refine your style, strengthen your descriptive powers, bring music to your words, and much more! *#10339/$14.95/304 pages*

The Writer's Digest Character Naming Sourcebook — Finally, you'll discover how to choose the perfect name to reflect your character's personality, ethnicity, and place in history. Here you'll find 20,000 first and last names (and their meanings) from around the world! *#10390/$18.95/352 pages*

The Writer's Essential Desk Reference — Why is it essential? Because it answers all the writing questions you face every day — book proposals, research techniques, overcoming writer's block and more. You'll refer to it again and again as you pursue your writing career. *#10243/$19.95/352 pages*